Fashion Décor

New Interiors for Concept Shops

GINGKO PRESS

FASHION DÉCOR
New Interiors for Concept Shops

Copyright © 2010 by SANDU PUBLISHING

First Published in the United States of America by Gingko Press
by arrangement with Sandu Publishing Co., Ltd.

Gingko Press, Inc.
1321 Fifth Street
Berkeley, CA 94710, USA
Tel: (510) 898 1195
Fax: (510) 898 1196
E-mail: books@gingkopress.com
www.gingkopress.com

Sponsored by: Design 360° — Concept and Design Magazine
www.360indesign.com
Chief Editor: Wang Shaoqiang
Executive Editor: Qingya Ke, Jingwei Yi
Chief Designer: Angel
Book Designer: Artemis Mai
Images on covers, contents and index courtesy of Havon Studio
Sales Manager:
Niu Guanghui (China), Daniela Huang (International)
Address:
3rd Floor, West Tower
No. 10 Ligang Road, Haizhu District
510280, Guangzhou, China
Tel: (86)-20-84344460
Fax: (86)-20-84344460
sandu84344460@163.com
www.sandu360.com

ISBN: 978-1-58423-384-8

Printed and bound in China

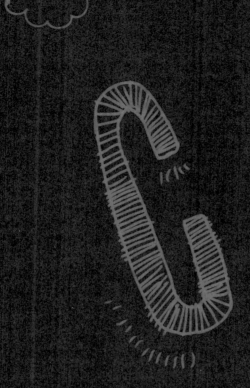

FOREWORD

by
Jeffrey Allsbrook &
Silvia Kuhle,
Standard

Presenting a worldwide collection of retail fashion stores, this book surveys what are perhaps global culture's most contemporary spaces. Fashion environments are the spatial representation of the moment, capturing the intersection between the physical world and a world dominated by images. Like the more mannered expressions of glamour magazines and the internet, fashion interiors are intended to capture the imagination while creating and fulfilling desire. While an engaging print ad is a mirror holding up an image of our dreams, fashion stores turn the mirror into a stage, inviting us into a world that is in perfect contrast to the usually messy context of commerce. As fashion commerce and consumption increasingly migrate to the web, paradoxically, retail spaces have become even more intense foci of brand identity. They exist, it seems, almost as if to prove that the image is real. But beyond their function as spaces of commerce, fashion interiors are collaborative works of applied art that often bring people from vastly different experiences together. They are individual sites of experimentation and invention, and as a whole, are a snapshot of our dynamic global culture.

As the calling cards for their style, brand's successful stores are multisense experiences. They are the setting to engage and persuade, to surround the client in the message. Competition at the forefront breeds necessity for invention, which in turn gives innovative design an edge, as well as a tangible value. Ostensibly environments for the display of merchandise, these spaces are crafted with the same tools as an exhibition of fine art. They engage the same territory as the gallery and the museum, which in turn increasingly seem to borrow from the environments of commerce. Where artists are commissioned to create specific works within retail stores, museums want to engage design in similarly compelling ways. For brands, the alchemy of positioning merchandise as art or design translates to equity, enhancing the aura and the perceived value of the apparel.

More and more these retail sequences are bringing apparel designers, architects and interior designers, graphic designers, product designers and artists together to create environments that in turn maximize effect. Whether it is a local boutique or a prototype for a larger environmental identity, fashion environments are opportunities to imagine and invent. As physical spaces, retail stores are meaningful precisely because of their temporality and scale. Often produced under impossibly tight schedules, they demand quick solutions with maximum impact. Not surprisingly, these conditions invite risk-taking and experimentation on the part of designers, but what is amazing is the sheer diversity and uniqueness of the resulting environments. Ranging from the detailed and graphic to the transparent to the simply dramatic to pure theater, the projects in this collection prove that working with one of the tiniest typologies — the shop — does not constrain creativity, but in fact tend to release it. New forms, techniques and materials as well as new uses for old materials frequently make their first expression in fashion environments, as the relatively small scale of the

projects makes another approaches feasible... ...reinforce strength... the designs is partially the result of the premise... collaboration between the fashion designer and the space designer, creating hybrids that challenge conventional ways of thinking.

The world of fashion commerce celebrates both... ...and the heterogeneity of contemporary space... are developing global signals while simultaneously defining distinctions through carefully designed ideas... ...brands in global culture, these spaces... expanding reach and multinational brands into new territories. It is... affirmation that fashion and design discourse does not recognize borders. The diversity of expression displayed on these pages is a reflection of the health and vitality of that continuing conversation. Fashion environments have become a significant means of cultural representation, reflecting trends in clothing, architecture, interior design and art as a method of communicating... reside precisely between the arts and commerce without taking sides. Their neutral position afford a certain freedom because... place where the investment in refinement and excess may actually pencil out.

CONTENTS

Conceptual

Thematic

Minimal

Decorative

Calvin Klein's Senior Vice President of Creative Services, Dale Rozmiarek, approached REX to design a concept house showcasing pieces from the company's apparel, accessory, and home lines. The catch: the house would be realized in miniature and displayed in the main window of Calvin Klein's Madison Avenue store during the 2008-2009 holiday seasons. REX named this fusion of concept house and doll house a "(Doll) House." For REX - a practice committed to using constraints as generative opportunities - the project was challengingly whimsical, presenting an exciting opportunity to test the limits of the firm's methodology across multiple scales. In keeping with Calvin Klein's aesthetic, the design began as four minimalist floor plates (dining room, living room, bedroom, and rooftop pool terrace). The plates were then shifted to maximize visibility into the doll house, and to provide views for the hypothetical occupant of the concept house. The resulting 450 kg (Doll) House was fabricated in steel and acrylic sheet and wrapped in a cocoon of white four-way stretch nylon fabric selected for its translucence and ability to shift from taut planes to soft curves as the side panels are opened and closed. The interiors and roof terrace were furnished with miniature replicas of pieces designed by Calvin Klein's creative directors: Francisco Costa, Calvin Klein Collection for Women; Italo Zucchelli, Calvin Klein Collection for Men; Ulrich Grimm, Calvin Klein Shoes & Accessories; and Amy Mellen, Calvin Klein Home.

MADISON AVENUE (DOLL) HOUSE

REX

Architect/ REX
Structure/ Magnusson Klemencic Associates
Fabrication/ Situ Studio
Client/ Calvin Klein, Inc.
Photography/ James Lattanzio
Site/ New York, US
Area/ 4 sqm
Date of Completion/ November 2008

The architects at Guise have been asked to develop a full scale retail concept, with a spatial language to correlate with the design philosophy of Fifth Avenue Shoe Repair. The full brief includes a concept store, shop-in-shops, a mobile fair interior and a pop-up store concept. First up is the pop-up store, a low cost retail experiment which will introduce the new spatial concept of Fifth Avenue Shoe Repair to the public.

The result is an entangled interior which aims to entice the customers to look further into the labyrinthine plan and discover the world of Fifth Avenue Shoe Repair. The main spatial ingredient is an over 2 km long woven belt, which is used to create the intertwined spaces. Custom made steel bars are placed around the store area to act as pillars on which to mount the belts. Embedded in the structure is the "by the no" collection. Around the walls clothes are hung in larger quantities. The clothes are revealed as people move along the structure. The belt is the main ingredient, both aesthetically and in quantity. The belt is delivered in rolls of 1000 m and is therefore very easy to transport. All the belts are being prepared at the office Guise, and delivered to the site in rolls. The logistic concept is "Retail space on a roll."

The shop-in-shop concept is to be implemented to carefully selected sales points internationally, to be followed by a concept store in central Stockholm.

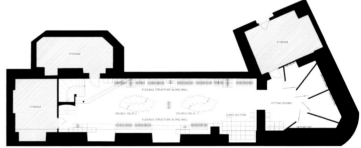

PLAN 1

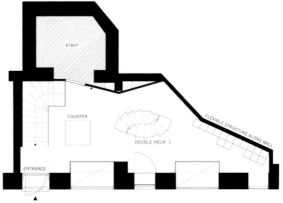

PLAN 0

FIFTH AVENUE SHOE REPAIR

Guise

Design/ Jani Kristoffersen & Andreas Ferm
Client/ Fifth Avenue Shoe Repair
Photography/ Lance & John, Mattias Lindbäck
Site/ Stockholm, Sweden
Area/ 150 sqm
Date of Completion/ 2009

Makoto Tanijiri of Suppose Design Office designed a store installation at the Diesel Denim Gallery in Aoyama, Tokyo. The concept of the installation is based on a single idea of "The Garden," a walk through nature, while the plastic plumbing pipe tree grows into the store. The idea is a plastic tree which has grown over time and has covered the store's ceiling and walls with its branches. An atmosphere like a natural axis is created in the space covered by artificial plumbing. The plumbing and the light effects give off amazing scenographic shadows on the wooden floors and the polished cement slab walls. The white plumbing pipes have an amazing contrast with the black ceiling when the visitor looks up to see the shapes that the growing branches form. The complex plumbing trails around the polished grey cement wall in all directions, making it hard for the human eye to follow the ever-growing branch. The new attractive scenery is presented with plumbing and fashion items to primarily show how functional objects, such as plumbing pipes, have diverse usage and a higher value when creativity gives these simple objects a whole new meaning. In the past, denim was primarily recognized as work clothing, but now it has become a high fashion item to many people. Plumbing similarly– becomes art when it is used in the "Nature Factory."

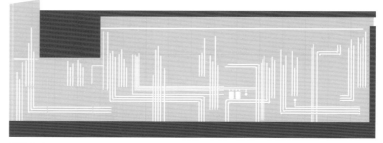

ELEVATION 1

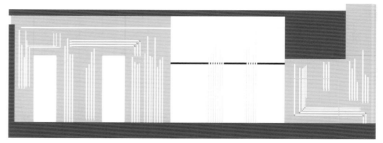

ELEVATION 2

NATURE FACTORY

Suppose Design Office

Design/ Makoto Tanijiri
Client/ Diesel Denim Gallery
Photography/ Toshiyuki Yano, Nacasa & Partners
Site/ Tokyo, Japan
Date of Completion/ August 2009

PLAN

TYPE-A TYPE-B TYPE-C TYPE-D FREE

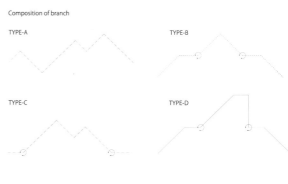

Composition of branch

TYPE-A   TYPE-B

TYPE-C   TYPE-D

Several kinds of basic shape is made from the rearrangement of the standard goods.

This is a flagship shop for a women's clothing brand called "EIFINI" which runs 180 shops in China.

In order to spotlight the clothes, the designers integrated the floor, walls, and ceiling by using the color white, so as to create a feeling of expansive space. Equipment, such as the counter, is designed in a very simple way, as if it is rising up from the tiled floor. A "pipe like hanger" of 250 meters laces through the space.

The "pipe" is supported by transparent acrylic rods from all directions, which make it look like it has been released from gravity and is floating freely through space. While maintaining the transparency of the space, the pipe transforms itself to divide up and create different scenes: by folding the pipe several times, a tunnel like entrance is formed; a display area is formed inside the whirlpool of the pipe; a fitting room can be created by simply hanging a curtain over the pipe. The distribution of these scenes enriches the entire space, which also makes it a diversified space. The track of the floating pipe looks like the trace drawn by the movement of a conductor's baton. The pipe emphasizes the presence of clothes, but at the same time, it manifests its own existence. As the concert goes on, the clothes and the pipe take turns at playing the lead. Visit this place and feel the melody of the orchestra. Each season, the melody changes.

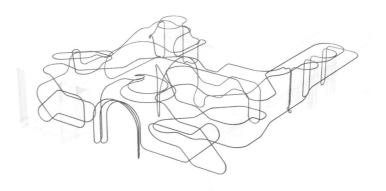

EIFINI

SAKO Architects

Design/ Keiichiro Sako, Ken-ichi Kurimoto, Liang Ju
Client/ EIFINI
Photography/ Misae Hiromatsu, Beijing NDC Studio, Inc.
Site/ Chengdu, China
Area/ 160 sqm
Date of Completion/ September 2008

The client's concept was a "Cultural Community Center." The designers focused on how the commercial space could co-exist with the public space. To make the space more open to those not familiar with design, art, or even the shop itself, the designers tried to blur the boundaries of inside and outside. The small wooden chair, a symbol of the community center, is attached to the wall and is on the door to the restroom. The jungle gym, a symbol of the park, is echoed in the creation of stairs and shelves. These plans are selected to convey the message of "Cultural Community Center" in a playful way, encouraging people to enjoy the space. Every detail contributes to the simplicity of the space. The division of the gallery space is created by the difference in floor heights. The chairs on the wall are to be taken off, which enables the gallery wall to become larger or smaller. The attention to the boundaries of the two spaces enables both functions, commercial and public, to exist in independent involvement.

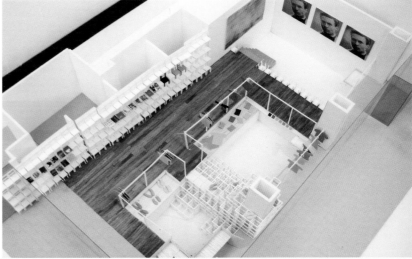

REED SPACE

upsetters architects

Design/ upsetters architects
Client/ Staple Design Studio/EIKO Shoji
Photography/ Yusuke Wakabayashi
Site/ Tokyo, Japan
Area/ 117.98 sqm
Date of Completion/ September 2006

The store is situated on two floors with large windows providing an easy vantage point into the space. Windows are not used in a typical showcase manner, but are instead used to guide the visitor's view through the space and spotlight dresses throughout the room. The space of the store was reorganized in order to emphasize structural elements. Simple walls and a few columns and beams are the main architectural elements. This space is part of broader research that the designers are undertaking, involving how imperceptible changes in space can modify behavior.

Furniture was designed by computer scripts, following a basic module, which repeats and switches the position. Curves of movement and actions, ergonomic needs, and lighting and views were all inserted in a 3D model to create a study of the space. The furniture was not designed to be repositioned, but is instead designed to visually function within the space as it was planned out.

Hanging bars playfully engage with the dresses and propose a way through the space, creating a trajectory of movement for the visitor. The bars turn around the viewing windows, leaving open space for exhibition, but also performing as a folding screen that will maintain the intimacy of the space. To reach the upper floor, the visitor crosses a narrow staircase built as a tunnel. The staircase is a mode of transit, within which visual superposition of both floors is impossible. Only the vivid memory of the floor below is possible. The floor treatment is made with large blocks of Travertino beige-grey natural stone that play in contrast to the material of the furniture. The entrance is at the lower-level, passing under a black canopy which is designed like a shadow-block over the door - a shadow without an object.

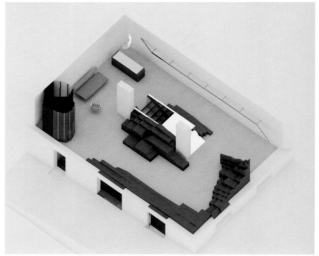

ANTONIOS MARKOS STORE

Gonzalez Haase / AAS

Design/ Pierre Jorge Gonzalez, Judith Haase
Client/ Antonios Markos
Photography/ Thomas Meyer/ Ostkreuz
Site/ Athens, Greece
Area/ 200 sqm
Date of Completion/ October 2009

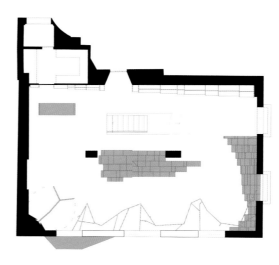

SOS is a Swedish skiwear brand, renowned for their bold use of colors. Initially the colors were used to clearly stand out in the monochrome white snowy landscapes. The shapes of the clothes, however, are modest, clean shapes which mainly aim to portray the functional aspects of the clothes themselves.

The design concept of the SOS Sportswear of Sweden Concept store derives from the clothes and the environment of their intended use. The interior is a complement to the clothes; the space and its furniture are monochrome and strong in shape so as to enhance the clothes and to resemble the skiing environment. The furniture has a simple square plan shape, but is cut in a steep angle to resemble the oblique surfaces found in nature. The angle of the top surface is as steep as possible, while still allowing garments to be placed without falling down. The very steep furniture, however, has large steel plates embedded behind the rubber surface, enabling the clothes to be pinned up on the surface using magnets.

Around the store large panels cover the walls. The panels are CNC-cut in a pattern resembling stems and branches.

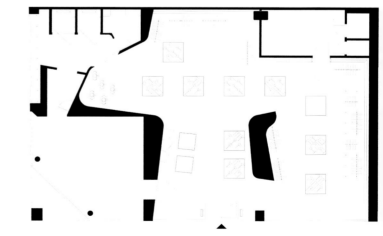

SOS FLAGSHIP STORE

Guise

Design/ Jani Kristoffersen, Andreas Ferm
Client/ SOS Sportwear
Photography/ Lance & John
Site/ Stockholm, Sweden
Area/ 240 sqm
Date of Completion/ 2009

William Russell has designed the new Alexander McQueen store in Los Angeles. The flagship shop is located on Melrose Avenue on the corner of Melrose Place and is the latest in a recent expansion by McQueen, which has seen Russell-designed stores opening in Las Vegas, Moscow, Bahrain, Osaka and Vilnius.

The store employs the interior design language created by Russell and McQueen for the three original Flagship Stores in London, Milan and New York, creating a branded spatial experience full of drama and intrigue.

The theatrical quality of the interior, inspired by McQueen's extraordinary catwalk shows, compliments the clothes while the limited palette of materials and precise detailing allow the collection to stand out.

The Los Angeles store is unique for two major reasons. Most importantly, because this was a new-build project on a vacant site, Russell was able, for the first time, to design the form of the exterior as well as the interior. Working closely with the landlord he has created a streamlined building in stucco and curved glass with a large private courtyard behind.

The second point of difference is the installation of a large sculpture by Robert Bryce Muir. Visitors to the store are greeted by the feet and legs of the piece, entitled "Angel of the Americas" suspended through a skylight above the entrance. With his head and shoulders outside the store, the figure appears to be levitating.

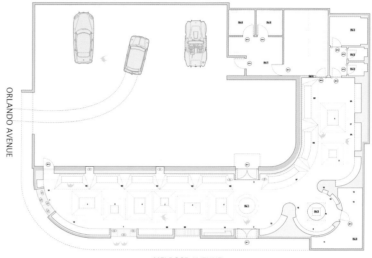

ALEXANDER MCQUEEN STORE

William Russell, Pentagram

Design/ William Russell
Client/ Alexander McQueen
Photography/ Benny Chan
Site/ Los Angeles, US
Date of Completion/ 2008

The design concept is based upon the incidence of light from the roof windows and the ceiling height. A hanger is placed under each roof window to display the Permanent Vacation Autumn/Winter collection. A wooden fan is pointed towards each hanger, making it rotate by using the garment as sails. Along the walls of the store different hangers display photos and selected pieces from the collection.

During the day, the only lighting in the space comes from daylight shining in through the windows. To retain that feeling during nighttime, artificial light sources are placed on the rooftop outside the windows shining in.

PERMANENT VACATION

1:2:3 & Kristoffer Sundin

Client/ Permanent Vacation
Photography/ 1:2:3
Site/ Gallery Nya Skolan Gothenburg
Date of Completion/ September 2009

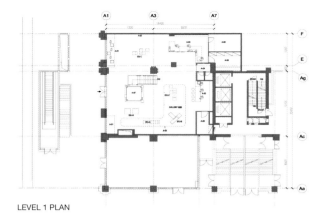

LEVEL 1 PLAN

LEVEL 2 PLAN

For the new Source Flagship Store in Beijing, the designers proposed a 9 meter high "Shoe Tower" at the entrance of the store, which could display the extensive shoe collection. The shoe tower was based on a concept of stacked shoeboxes - which functions as the main display feature and as a staircase connecting the two floors of the store. The Tetris-like form of the tower is comprised of shifting boxes that are literally stacked with some left open and others made of glowing light boxes.

The design of the overall racking system is based on a fashion warehouse distribution centre where clothes racks can be easily manually moved around on skids. Some skids are also used for displaying artwork during exhibitions held in the store and for clothing.

The wall display pieces are also modular and clamp onto the metal mesh wall grid structure, which allows for total flexibility and manipulation by the visual merchandiser. The display boxes are shaped in "L" and "T" shapes in the theme of the building blocks of the shoe tower.

The second floor also features two "Shoe Walls" in the men and women's sections, each with over 70 standardized L-shaped shoe display elements, which are shifting in different directions to create curved and wave effects.

SOURCE FLAGSHIP STORE

HUGE *Architects*

Design/ Samuel Tsang, Victor Njo, Betty Zhong, Renkin Yin, Gerald Russelman, Maling, Xu Chun Ming, Jeff Luo
Client/ Source
Photography/ Source Tsang
Site/ Gala Place, Beijing, China
Area/ 800 sqm
Date of Completion/ August 2009

As part of a complete rebranding effort, the shop concept is a modern and sexy solution designed to propel this Italian knitwear label in a completely new direction and firmly into the future of retail.

The components, mainly gloss lacquered GRP and polished stainless steel, are fabricated off site and come together fluidly to form the walls, display surfaces and furniture, creating the impression of a continuous form moulded into display props and surfaces. The sense of composition is reinforced by the attention paid to the smallest detail. The motif of square into circle repeats throughout, from the curvy rectangles of the wall units and freestanding furniture to the bespoke stools, shelves and door handles. The language is incorporated into stylized mannequins and hangers and is echoed in the minimalism of the window vitrines.

Stefanel's complicated knitwear designs don't display to their full potential on standard mannequins, or even stay on them properly. The solution to it was a bespoke design contoured with flocking material which holds the garments in place and brings their detailing into view. By providing non-slip functionality in such a graphic and recognizable way, a display prop moves beyond its obvious functionality to enhance brand identity.

The design provides the client with complete flexibility and future expandability. Selecting from a wide range of components, the kit can be customized to suit shop locations of any size and budget and can be easily and cost-effectively installed on site in a matter of days. Every surface offers a means of display, which can be as dense or as sparse as necessary. Merchandising can change by season or collection and the system's modularity easily permits both the addition of extra components and the development of new ones, ensuring the concept can adapt to meet future needs and evolve along with the brand.

STEFANEL

Sybarite (UK)

Client/ Stefanel, Italy
Photography/ Marco Zanta
Site/ Frankfurt, Germany
Area/ 248 sqm
Date of Completion/ September 2009

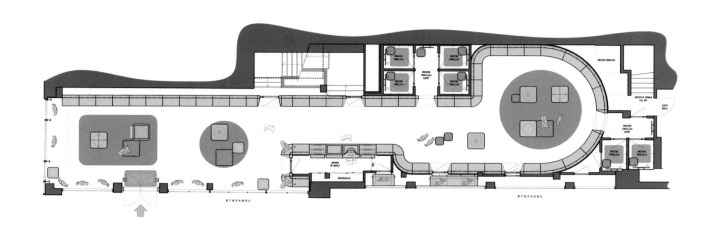

The space has an exhibitions floor and storage space in the mezzanine, in addition to the ground floor. This store sits in the Daikanyama district and looks like a box. The perimeter of the facade is 18 linear meters and 6.5 meters high and wraps the four sides of the building. The construction work was finished in two months. The facade is made of Formica covered with prints that are updated every season, following the graphics of the current collection. When the box is closed, it inspires curiosity. When it is opened, the interior is not completely visible. Inside, the focus is on the hanger installations, where an acrylic finish, fluorescent bulbs, and tiles turn into great product support.

ALEXANDRE HERCHCOVITCH

Studio Arthur Casas

Client/ Alexandre Herchcovitch
Photography/ Studio Arthur Casas
Site/ Tokyo, Japan
Area/ Basement, 315.93 sqft/
1st Floor, 315.93 sqft/ Mezzanine area, 131.43 sqft
Date of Completion/ 2007

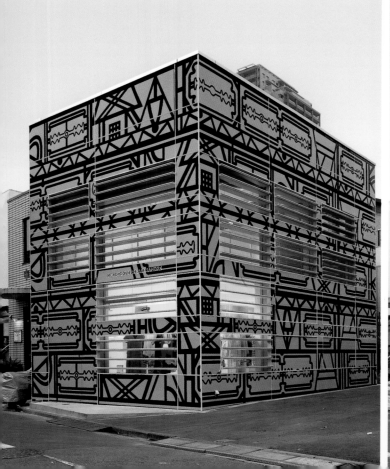

The design for the Delicatessen clothing store follows the economical logic of fashion design. Two main strategies were brought in from the world of fashion and introduced into the space: the use of transient materials and the idea of a disjointed layer that would cover the space.

The means of production were appropriated from the economy of fashion design. A thin, raw and transient material, the pegboard, was draped over the space. By cutting, folding, revealing and wrapping, the original purpose of the material is transformed to create the display elements, fitting room, desk and store front. By mounting the pegboard on the entire 5m high space, and lighting it from behind, this rough hardware store material turned into an ephemeral, lace-like dress that wraps around the space. The grid of holes, made for hooks, was transformed into a garment pattern. These holes can either act as a display apparatus or they can hold the bare hooks which produce a three dimensional fabric.

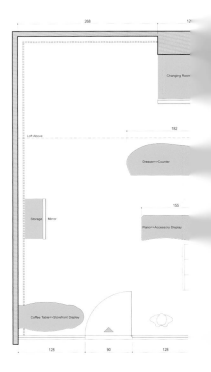

DELICATESSEN

Z-A Studio

Design/ Dan Affleck, Adam Hostetler, Leo Mulvehill, Guy Zucker
Client/ Idit Barak
Photography/ Assaf Pinchuk
Site/ Masaryk Square, Tel Aviv
Area/ 35 sqm
Date of Completion/ 2009

The designer used the vertical lines of the premises as the basis for the structure of the design. The column that has replaced the partition wall stands exactly on the intersection of the floor plan. The steel supporting beam has been covered from floor to ceiling with mirrors. The entire shop space can be seen through the mirrors. Customers are able to use the mirror to try on shoes. Since only the bottom 90 cm are covered in mirrors, these heavy structural features seem to float in space.

There are two patches of stainless steel rods with artistic shoes perched on top of them like colorful butterflies. The rods are firmly anchored in a fixed grid. The shoes are attached by strong magnets. This symbolic design is a kind of monument to the memory of the late Richard Hermans Jr., one of the initiators of Kymyka. The tubes, in different lengths, symbolize altar candles, and offer insiders a moment of comfort.

An all-in-one wall unit of multi-functional console tables surrounds the space and is intriguing and stylish. The beams also embrace the room, keeping the irregular shape of the floor plan together through their linear simplicity. All interior elements are tailor-made, including the wooden console tables. The light fittings on the ceiling were also designed especially for Kymyka. The lamps can be turned and tilted in all directions and can therefore be turned to light up all walls, console tables and tube patches, in every product arrangement imaginable. The light reflection is reminiscent of a halo, adding a little extra mystical feel.

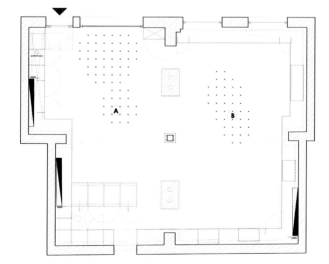

KYMYKA

Maurice Mentjens Design

Client/ Kymyka, Maastricht
Photography/ Arjen Schmitz
Site/ Maastricht, the Netherlands
Area/ 77 sqm
Date of Completion/ January 2009

This project is a show room and prototype store for a new women's clothing brand. It is located within the brand's design studio and clothing factory, situated close to the entryway and formerly used as a fabrication studio. The design goal was to respond to the client's desire to serve the stylish, confident and still feminine career woman.

The "L-Container" functions dually as a spatial volume and a separation element. The floor inside was lifted to represent a stage. The "L-Container" introduces a contoured alleyway to recall the sensation of a private walk-in-closet at home, which is the real stage for actual people. A convertible dressing room places real women at the center of the deepened "display window," which projects directly toward the entryway and traverses the whole store. Gray tiles pave the catwalks penetrating the "L-container," weaving between the public and private space. This composition of the store's circulation creates the visual and physical connections between all areas essential in a retail establishment.

The two-way hanger system creates a vivid red belt, continually lacing through lighted wall niches around the room. CNC technology was used to pre-fabricate materials such as the flooring and resin panels, while thousands of beads were arrayed by hand to create a crystal curtain with the store logo patterned within.

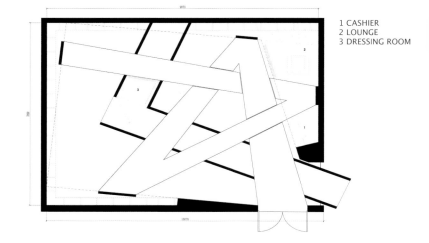

1 CASHIER
2 LOUNGE
3 DRESSING ROOM

WOMEN'S CLOTHING STORE, SONG MAX

Elevation Workshop

Design/ Na Wei
Client/ Song Max
Photography/ Elevation Workshop, JR & other media
Site/ Beijing, China
Area/ 78 sqm
Date of Completion/ August 2009

There is a small two-story house which was built a half century ago, and about forty years ago a wooden hut with a gable roof was built onto the terrace of the house. The project was to make the hut on the terrace into an office and showroom. The terrace hadn't had any plants for forty years, and was originally unplanned, with both large and small frame elements such as beams and pillars. The designer realized that the hut could be a unique object. After providing structural reinforcement, the designer pursued a thorough space arrangement by covering all the surfaces, including floors, walls, and garrets, with symmetrical flooring materials painted gray. The framework painted white runs through the space within this gable roofed hut. This is a garret office and showroom where only the history of the hut itself and the clothes are put on display.

DOUBLE OO 96

CASE-REAL

Design/ Koichi Futatsumata
Client/ alohanine
Photography/ Hiroshi Mizusaki
Site/ Fukuoka, Japan
Area/ 36.3 sqm
Date of Completion/ 2009

FIRST FLOOR PLAN

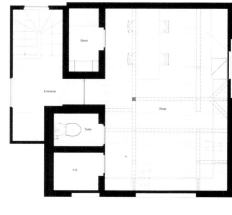

SECOND FLOOR PLAN

BOUTIQUE BALI BARRET

Franklin Azzi Architecture

Client/ Bali Barret Japan / Sazaby Inc.
Photography/ Franklin Azzi Architecture
Site/ Tokyo, Japan
Date of Completion/ September 2004

Boutique Bali Barret includes two projects: the Red Bunker and the Red Military Tent. The Red Bunker 01 project in Tokyo projects a radical image. It takes a type of architecture out of its context, as bunkers were mainly built along the Atlantic coast during the Second World War. Usually, each bunker was named-often after a woman, such as Barbara and Karola. This one is called Bali Barret. In this project, the red facade acts as a landmark, a point of reference throughout the city. This Bali idea of a "red shop" is simply achieved by painting the bunker in red. The opacity of the concrete facade and the lack of information about what resides inside increases the curiosity of passers-by. The three facades of the red bunker are slightly tilted to symbolize the change of gravity. Inside the shop, one finds the traditional defense system of the bunker, with its loopholes-one opening onto the main street, the second one onto the secondary street and the third one onto the beveled edge. There are small crenels with very little visibility, through which one observes the immediate surroundings in a small space with a low ceiling.

The project of the Red Military Tent 02 is another radical image based on the archetype of military tents. The textile is initially beige or khaki, but is suddenly transformed into a red canvas, as if through the master stroke of an artist. The main idea is to project an architectural archetype outside of its initial geographic context, toward the street and the city. By playing on the imagination, the object of fiction is revealed. Once away from its initial space, the object reflects a sideways image that moves the surrounding urban space. The project is made up of a facade of red oiled fabric, which is held by natural leather straps and suspended by a metallic structure. This fabric is held at the bottom by sand bags. The entrance is through a metallic chamber.

NO MATTER
WHERE
YOU GO
THERE
YOU ARE

Thematic 072

This redesign project has been carried out based on conservation of the interior, which Tokujin Yoshioka had previously designed by using recycled aluminum material initially developed as auto parts. Issey Miyake's concept is to reincarnate the space as "Pleats Please Issey Miyake / Aoyama" by conserving the existing space with recycled aluminum in order to have it transcend time. The designer proposed to use a huge lighting wall. The lighting wall serves to accentuate the nature of the material and interfuses modern technology and light.

PLEATS PLEASE
ISSEY MIYAKE

Tokujin Yoshioka Design

Design/ Tokujin Yoshioka
Client/ Issey Miyake
Photography/ Tokujin Yoshioka Design
Site/ Aoyama, Japan
Area/ 220 sqm
Date of Completion/ September 2009

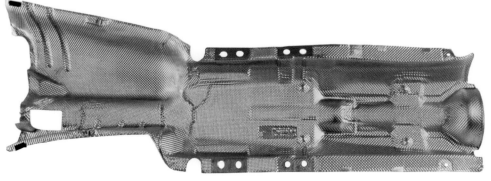

The STUSSY shop project faces the street in a central Fukuoka urban area. The space is made up of natural Bianco Carrara marble. By refining the space using white marble, the designer aimed to project a new image of street fashion by mixing street culture with classical imagery.

STUSSY
FUKUOKA CHAPT

CASE-REAL

Design/ Koichi Futatsumata
Client/ DICE&DICE
Photography/ Hiroshi Mizusaki
Site/ Fukuoka,Japan
Date of Completion/ 2009

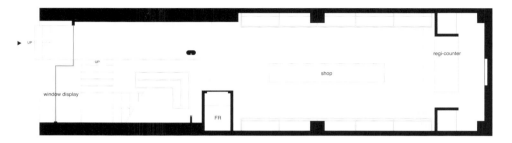

The groundbreaking 35,000 square foot Barbie Flagship for Mattel holds the world's largest and most comprehensive collection of Barbie dolls and licensed Barbie products, as well as a range of services and activities for Barbie fans and their families.

Mattel wanted a store where "Barbie is the hero" and where Barbie is expressed as a global lifestyle brand by building on the brand's historical link to fashion. Barbie Shanghai is the first fully realized expression of this broader vision. It is a sleek, fun, unapologetically feminine interpretation of Barbie: past, present, and future.

For the new façcde, the designers combined references to product packaging, decorative arts, fashion and architectural iconography to create a modern identity for the store, expressing Barbie's cutting-edge fashion sense and history.

The façade is made of two layers: molded, translucent polycarbonate interior panels and flat exterior glass panels printed with a whimsical lattice pattern. The two layers reinforce each other visually and interact dynamically through reflection, shadow, and distortion.

Upon entry, visitors are enveloped by curvaceous, pearlescent surfaces of the lobby, leading to a pink escalator tube that takes them from the bustle of the street, to the double-height main floor.

The central feature within the store is a three-story spiral staircase enclosed by eight hundred Barbie dolls. The staircase and the dolls are the core of the store; everything literally revolves around Barbie. The staircase links the three retail floors: the women's floor (women's fashion, couture, cosmetics, and accessories); the doll floor (dolls, the designer doll gallery, doll accessories, books) featuring the Barbie Design Center, where girls design their own Barbie; and the girls' floor (girls' fashion, shoes, and accesories). The Barbie Fashion Stage is also on this floor, where girls take part in a real runway show. The Barbie Cafe is on the top floor.

Throughout the retail areas, the designers played with the scale differences between dolls, girls, and women. They reinforced the feeling of youth and the possibilities of an unapologetically girlish outlook (regardless of age) by mixing reality and fantasy and keeping play and fun at the forefront - creating a space where optimism and possibility reign supreme as expressions of core Barbie attributes.

BARBIE SHANGHAI

Slade Architecture

Client/ Mattel
Photography/ Iwan Baan
Site/ Shanghai, China
Area/ 2,790 sqm
Date of Completion/ March 2009

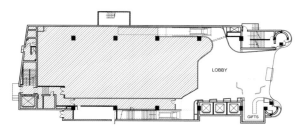

GROUND FLOOR PLAN

THIRD FLOOR PLAN

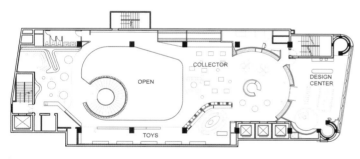

FOURTH FLOOR PLAN

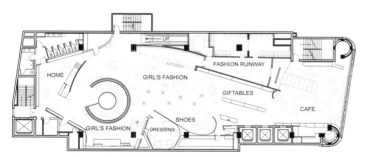

FIFTH FLOOR PLAN

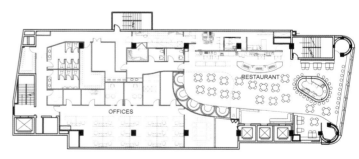

SIXTH FLOOR PLAN

This new project for Camper is inspired by classic circus elements. It has color and fantasy. The result is a space full of life and light that invites people to dream. As soon as people step through the impressive door of organic shapes, with a handle shaped like a candy cane, they begin to discover the surprises that await inside. For starters, there are no corners, only curved forms. There is an interesting contrast between the walls covered in Bisazza mosaic tiles, perfect and delicate, and the cement floor, basic and unfinished. The long, narrow centre table resembles a centipede. The colored mirrors placed on the ceiling elongate perspective and give the store added warmth. These small touches of quality do not go unnoticed. The special areas are separated by beveled glass panels reminiscent of cut gemstones. Color filters create a magical transparency. The shop is fresh and elegant.

CAMPER SHOP, TOKYO

Hayón Studio

Design/ Jaime Hayón
Client/ Camper
Photography/ Hayón Studio
Site/ Omotesando Dori, Tokyo
Date of Completion/ 2009

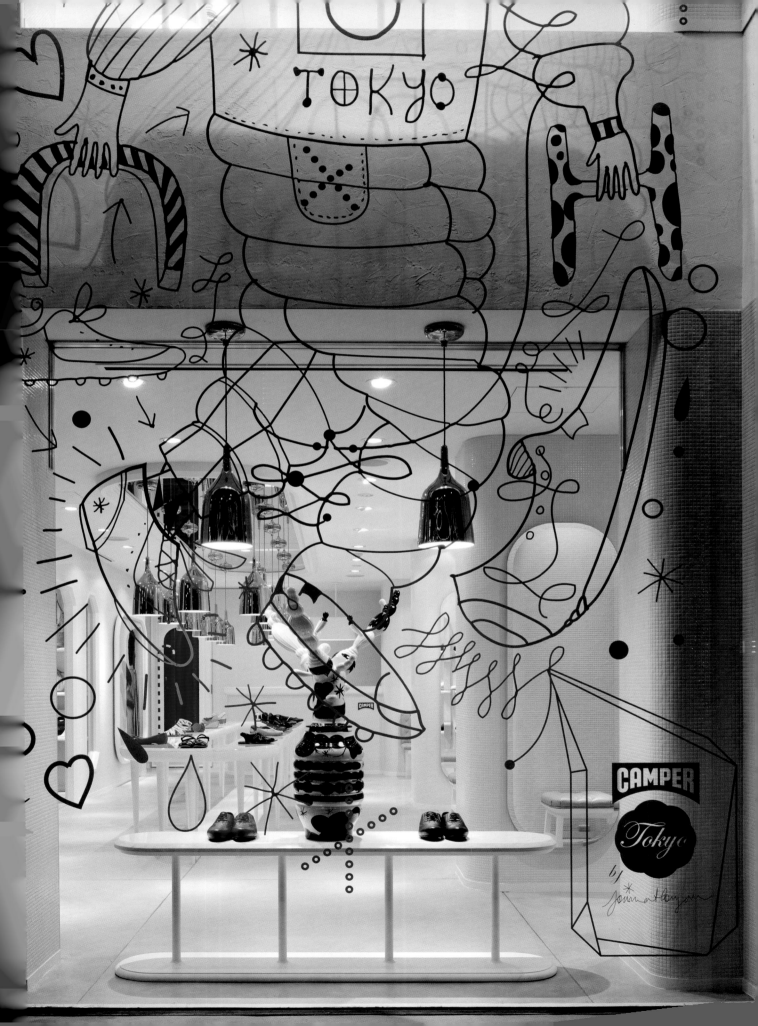

The intention of the Together project was to give an absolute yet subtle change to the way the Camper space is envisioned. Very special pieces were created in order to turn the shop into a symbol of elegance. Handmade wood tables were made with many different legs, which is very much within the Hayón style. A set of hand crafted terra-cotta lamps was designed specifically for the space. A new technology was developed to give these lamps an earthy, yet sophisticated surface. For the cash point space, the designer created an unusual piece of furniture with a very "Olympic" shape, all in red. The designer also chose a red floor in a silky and glossy resin that playfully contrasts with the rest of the space.

CAMPER TOGETHER

Hayón Studio

Design/ Jaime Hayón
Client/ Camper
Photography/ Nienke Klunder
Site/ Barcelona, Spain
Date of Completion/ 2007

CAMPER
together
with
Jaime Hayon
04
Episode

In the Camper showroom in Rome, tricycles weave through the shop. The interior "street" is decorated with mini traffic signs illustrated by Alfredo Häberli. Airplane-like lights give a sense of open air space, but actually the street is inside. The Camper shoes are presented on the "street."

CAMPER SHOWROOM, ROME

Alfredo Häberli

Client/ Camper
Photography/ Alfredo Häberli Design Development
Site/ Rome, Italy
Area/ 55 sqm
Date of Completion/ 2008

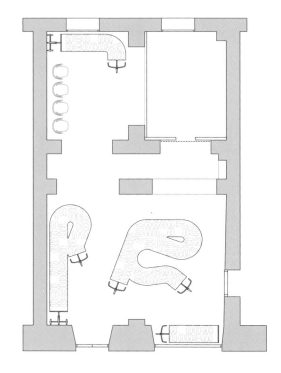

The display in the showroom is like a catwalk
show. The lights are luminous trousers, which
also take on the look of models presenting
the newest Camper shoes on the panels.

CAMPER
SHOWROOM,
PARIS

Alfredo Häberli

Client/ Camper
Photography/ Alfredo Häberli Design
Development
Site/ Paris, France
Area/ 50 - 55 sqm
Date of Completion/ 2009

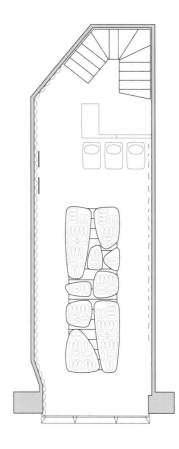

The black Uniqlo concept space is a place where people only see the branding and the products on display. Much of the store is in black, with walls and ceiling running into each other. During the design process, it was a challenge to choose elements and materials that would disappear or be combined with other elements, in order to make the colorful products pop out.

The redesign of the logo makes it stronger. A large "U" visible from the distance becomes a strong visual element. It is also used as a motif for the counter (which is actually half a "U" recreated by a mirror). The lighting on the ceiling was selected as it is reminiscent of the "O" of the logo. So the shop becomes a unique visual composition of the brand identity.

UNIQLO KIOSK
Curiosity

Design/ Gwenael Nicolas
Client/ Uniqlo
Photography/ Nacasa & Partenrs
Site/ Osaka, Japan
Area/ 140 sqm
Date of Completion/ 2006

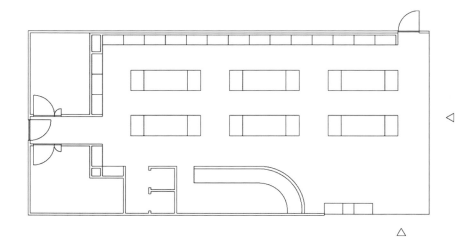

The new retail space of Uniqlo in Ginza is not just a shop but a new street. The front windowless facade is fully open to the outside. The space is rendered iconic by the graphic of crossing lines on the floor that invites the customer to cross the street and enter the space. The fluidity between the public space and retail environment is an attempt to redefine the code of retail. The graphic on the floor guides the customer through the shop in a seamless movement. The street is designed as if a series of kiosk shops are placed on the side of the road. The lighting creates the feeling of being outside in the middle of the afternoon.

Uniqlo's new design is an evolution of retail design using civic and cognitive symbols, an international language with which to create direct communication between the brand and customer, in order to create a unique and direct shopping experience.

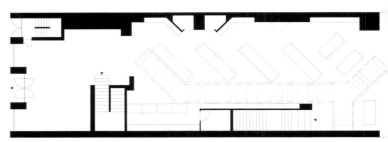

UNIQLO GINZA STREET

Curiosity

Design/ Gwenael Nicolas
Client/ Uniqlo
Photography/ Nacasa & Partenrs
Site/ Tokyo, Japan
Area/ 275 sqm
Date of Completion/ 2009

The façade is composed of two surfaces with geometrical lit lines. The lines make the materiality of the façade and architecture disappear so that only the Uniqlo logos remain within the complex maze of neon and information that Tokyo becomes at night. The layout and angulation of the towers blur the boundaries between the street and the retail space, creating a unique environment in a busy street of Shinjuku.

As the visitor moves freely around the three towers, the city becomes human scale. The vertical displays of the entrance are reflected on the mirrored wall, creating an amazing display gallery. The tower seems to be inserted into the interior of the shop within a maze of reflections. The challenge of the interior is for it not to "exist." Only the clothes are immediately visible. Display furniture is not only reduced to the minimum, but is also "designed" to be non-existent with materials selected for their immateriality. A lighting ceiling display and counters work together to remove the shadows of displays, creating an abstract retail environment where products and customers seem to float within a white glow.

UNIQLO MEGA STORE

Curiosity

Design/ Gwenael Nicolas
Client/ Uniqlo
Photography/ Nacasa & Partners
Site/ Tokyo, Japan
Area/ 3,040 sqm
Date of Completion/ 2009

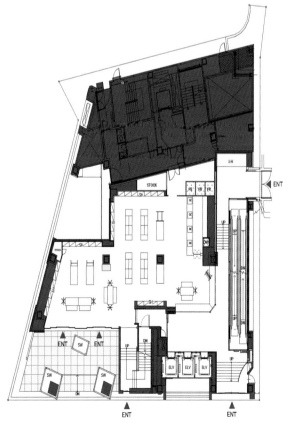

Subzero, FrontRunner's outlet for the luxury segment, has opened its doors on Amsterdam's main tourist gateway, the Damrak.

To catch the eye of the stream of tourists passing by its doors - amidst the visual cacophony of the surrounding souvenir shops - Subzero makes a bold statement in the shape of a dynamic wall consisting of backlit translucent boxes. Just one look will unmistakably tell you: this is a sneaker store.

Just as the dividing line between sports and fashion is fading, Subzero manages to combine the atmospheres of both gym and club: a rubber floor is dissected by colorful swirls; dark walls are horizontally crossed by stripes that happen to be dotted here and there. Also in the mix are white pendular lighting, color-changing LEDs in between a three stories high urban graphic, super-tall bronze coated mirror walls, chrome finished pin spots and white leather couches.

Then there is the basement. It is finished - ceiling and floor and all - in the sort of red you only find in nightclubs of the luxurious kind. It is the decor in which very exclusive designer sneakers are presented in strongly lit sculptural showcases.

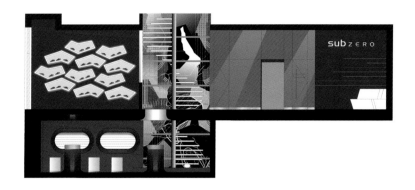

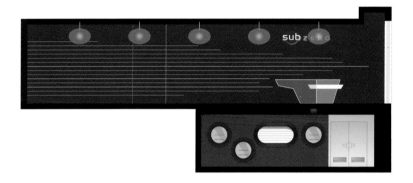

SUBZERO

Dastro Retailconcepts

Client/ FrontRunner
Photography/ Wim van Gelderen, Patrick Meis
Site/ Amsterdam, the Netherlands
Area/ 105 sqm
Date of Completion/ February 2008

① STAIRS
② STORAGE
③ ELEVATOR
④ FITTING ROOM
⑤ SEATING
⑥ GLASS
⑦ CASHDESK
⑧ CABINET
⑨ INSTALLATIONS

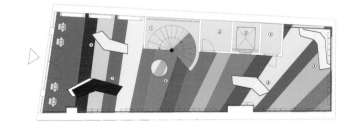

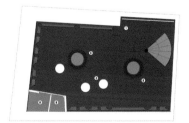

GROUND FLOOR

BASEMENT

The project, developed by Deardesign Studio, transmits the values and the philosophy of Munich Brand through an original and fresh ambience inspired by natural elements.

This Munich Flagship store is located in the shopping center L'illa Diagonal in Barcelona. Munich Fashion Division strongly emphasized its products and philosophy. Dark glass surfaces, mirrors, metal trees and cage-like boxes hanging from the ceiling recreate a carefree, experimental and impermanent atmosphere. The angular and clunky space with its hard edges and seemingly moving parts gave the store a playful, skate-style look.

One of the aims of the Brand was to create a comfortable and a pleasant space for consumers. The Studio paid attention to the decorative details and created the sensation of freedom within the environment. Everything is designed to be carefree, experimental, and timeless.

The new Flagship store clearly underlines that the 70 year old brand will always be "avant garde."

MUNICH FLAGSHIP STORE

Deardesign Studio

Design/ Ignasi Llauradó, Eric Dufourd, Dorien Peeters
Client/ Munich Sports
Photography/ Lafotográfica
Site/ Barcelona, Spain
Area/ 54 sqm
Date of Completion/ March 2009

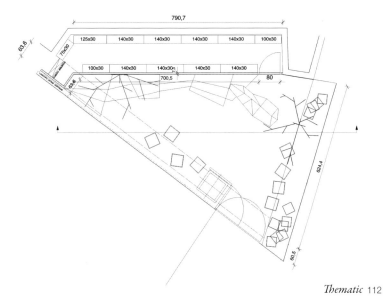

Munich Sports presented its new collection for its sport division in Ispo Winter Fair 2009, in Munich, Germany. The main idea of the booth was to present the product in a virtual catwalk. The Studio recreated the effect of shoes passing through the stand by LCD screens.

The catwalk presentation on a luminous stage was the central piece, where "flying shoes" were hung by XXL laces from a lighting box. The use of the laces allows the customers to easily take and touch the shoes.

In association with Moritz, the traditional Beer Brand from Barcelona, Munich mounted a lounge beer bar where people can have a drink and eat "Tapas." The booth reflects this lounge ambience and directly focuses on the product with smooth lighting effects.

Totally neutral wall panels serve to enhance the product and make it more attractive. All furniture is removable and creates various informal meeting spaces. On the façade, a huge lighting box announced the promotional campaign for 2009 and XXL laces repetitions created a multi-color see-through curtain wall near the entrance.

MUNICH ISPO 09

Deardesign Studio

Design/ Ignasi Llauradó, Eric Dufourd, Dorien Peeters
Client/ Munich Sports
Photography/ Julian Rupp
Site/ Munich, Germany
Area/ 60 sqm
Date of Completion/ May 2009

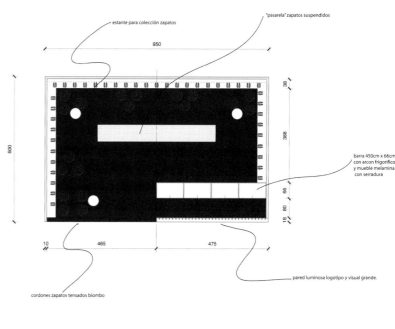

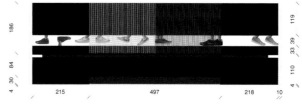

The project is a boutique in a multi-tenanted building facing the street. By placing a seven meter wide window on the back wall of the building, the designer transformed a closed place into a much different comfortable space. Once the visitor steps inside the shop, the outside cityscape appears through the wide window.

MA SHOP

CASE-REAL

Design/ Koichi Futatsumata
Client/ Font Co., Ltd.
Photography/ Hiroshi Mizusaki
Site/ Fukuoka, Japan
Area/ 40.8 sqm
Date of Completion/ 2005

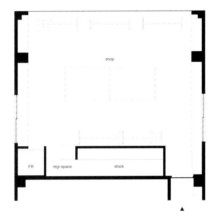

"The second façade" is a project in a tenant building facing a downtown street. This district faces an external common passage and its frontage is divided in two. The outside wall design was not appropriate for the image of the boutique and its brands, so a new outer wall was constructed inside of the lease line as a new shop façade. The earth floor "Doma" becomes the outside of the shop when it is opened. The new façade runs straight and considers the depth of the building opening, emphasizing the existence of the shop and its poetic dissonance within the space.

NOTE

CASE-REAL

Design/ Koichi Futatsumata
Client/ Very Inc.
Photography/ Hiroshi Mizusaki
Site/ Oita, Japan
Area/ 60.5 sqm
Date of Completion/ 2006

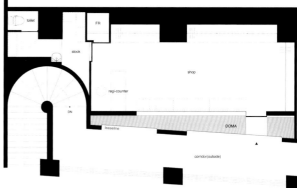

Fashion brand ASOBIO's first storefront shop designed by Nendo consists of a spacious bi-level interior with a generous opening. Keeping with the shop's theme "focus" - the designer positioned monotone photographs on the floor and walls, and varied the size to imitate the effect of a camera's zoom lens. The sharpness was also varied to recall the sense of being out of focus. These effects enhance the space with depth and continuity, provide variety and make the products on display stand out by appearing "in focus" in contrast to the shop's own patterns.

ASOBIO CHANNEL ONE

Nendo

Client/ ASOBIO
Photography/ Jimmy Cohrssen
Site/ Shanghai, China
Date of Completion/ June 2009

Kiki 2 is the outlet shop of Kiki Niesten in Maastricht. An outlet shop always reminds people of a warehouse or storage room. Kiki wanted a functional yet subtly chic and luxurious but witty shop interior, something with a sense of humor. It required a lot of storage space in the fairly small shop with a high ceiling. The shop is located in the Stokstraat in a 16th century building, in the heart of Maastricht. The shop is designed as a warehouse with walls and ceiling covered with racks/cabinets in grey oak wood, which looks a little old and dusty. The floor is covered with white clothes scattered across the floor and cast in completely transparent epoxy resin. It looks as if a client in a state of "shopping delirium" pulled everything out of the cabinets. Light shines down from a box over the counter, which conceals the staircase leading to the first floor. The door to this staircase is hidden behind a secret door at the left hand side of the counter, concealed behind the cabinets with mirrors at the back. A large glass walled cabinet next to the counter acts as a barrier to the back of the counter and blocks the direct draft when the front door is open. At the rear of the shop two dressing rooms are fitted into the cabinet walls on the same side as the counter. It is possible to hang clothing from three separate levels and shelves can be placed in all cabinets. Finally two ladders with the same wood finish as the cabinets were made to reach the higher shelves. Two special rods with a hook on the end were also made for this purpose.

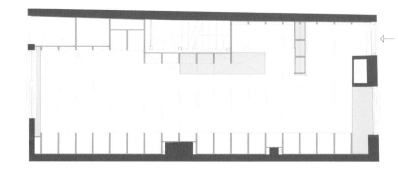

KIKI 2

Maurice Mentjens Design

Client/ Kiki Niesten
Photography/ Arjen Schmitz
Site/ Maastricht, the Netherlands
Area/ 34 sqm
Date of Completion/ 2006

A glowing glass corner above a floating display window announces the presence of Jenni Kayne's debut retail store, while the interior design modulates the space of the 2,400 square foot warehouse with a rhythmic series of walls and a soft palette of wood and brushed brass. An umbrella-like ceiling of thin cedar slats floats over the store, subtly integrating lighting and air circulation. Custom vitrines, tables and mirrors are focal elements of the design, variously combining brass, bamboo, smoked glass, and lacquered wood. The building's existing materials are exposed and integrated into the design. The concrete floors are ground and stained black steel beams are left unfinished, and the building's brick perimeter walls are painted white.

JENNI KAYNE

Standard

Design/ Jeffrey Allsbrook, Alexander Babich, Travis Muroki, Jaime Roveri
Client/ Jenni Kayne
Photography/ Benny Chan
Site/ Los Angeles, US
Area/ 2,400 sqft
Date of Completion/ November 2008

Situated in Ogilvy's, the Raffinati boutique took its
conceptual inspiration from the folding and unfolding
of the garment. First, a horizontal pliage holds the main
garment area and its changing rooms. Second, a vertical
intervention holds the second garment area as well as the
service point of this high end shop.

The general impact is one of purity. A myriad of whites is
used. The principal circulation volume is in a glossy finish
that allows for a reflection of the user. On the opposite
side, the principal shopping area has a more matte and
architectural feel in order to soften the clothing of this
line that caters to women. The garments are suspended
on sculptural and airy structures leaving the floor of this
600 square foot space empty of any clutter.

The lighting refines the feel of this space and leaves its
emphasis on the product. Finally a tableau of shadows
is created by the metal structures, a sort of textile weave
for a line of clothing that is bringing youth back to its
drawing table.

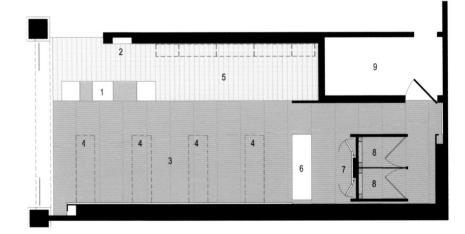

RAFFINATI

blazysgérard

Client/ Raffinalla
Photography/ Steve Montpetit
Site/ Montreal, Canada
Area/ 55 sqm
Date of Completion/ Spring 2008

Cenerino is a children's clothing store. The store concept has been developed through analyzing functionality, perception and the semantic aspect. It is a view of the children's world through an adult perspective. Over sized toys were used as pieces of furniture. The designer raised the level of the pavement through a ramp and thin steps to raise the importance of small objects. The space, which used to be long and narrow, was properly repartitioned.

Behind the colored mirror are fitting rooms, which hints at the game of hide-and-seek.

Long luminous shelves along the walls expand the space, illuminate and support the clothing and toys.

Rose colored window glass mixes with the external light and the blue of the walls. All of these elements come together to create a space with subtle reminders of childhood.

CENERINO

Andrea Tognon Architecture

Client/ Vittorio Cenere
Photography/ Cristian Guizzo
Site/ Bassano, Italy
Date of Completion/ March 2007

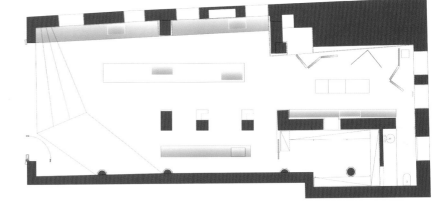

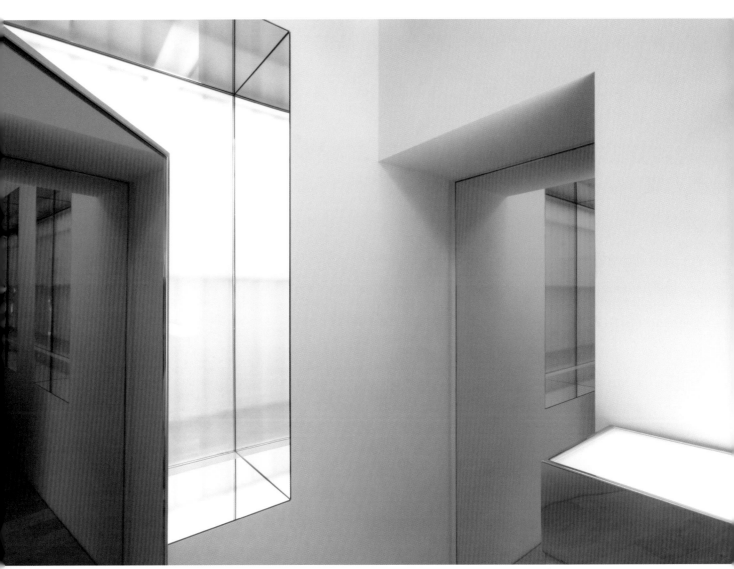

HIRSHLEIFER'S SHOE STORE

Sergio Mannino Studio

Design/ Mannino, Bruni, Scalettaris, Spagrud
Client/ Hirshleifer's
Photography/ Massimiliano Bolzonella
Site/ New York, US
Area/ 102 sqm
Date of Completion/ December 2008

The store is a subtle reference and homage to the world of art and design history, mainly Italian and American.

It is indeed a space where references and memories happen in a metaphysical way and are not entirely visible at first sight, a place for a dialogue between two opposite texts: the first is minimalist, rigorous and precise, alluding to the art of several American figures such as Sol LeWitt, Carl Andre or Donald Judd in its physicality and spirituality; the second is a reference to the rich, sensual, decadent, unpredictable and free world of the Radical Design groups that changed the course of design in Italy from the late sixties to the eighties.

Sergio Mannino negotiates masterfully between the tendencies of each "text" - style - to create surprising effects that contain continuity within the contradictions.

Space and timing are experienced through a proscenium of subtle humor and strict precision.

The rigorous formalism of the minimalists (whose formal precision is also easily found in the obsessive care for the details typical of the Italian culture) is challenged by "folies," unexpected elements winking at the viewer from some other world: a glass case sitting on a sofa (a reference to a 1967 piece by Italian Architect Gio Ponti); a neon sculpture gently curved but burning in white artificial light (another reference to the Italian art world of the sixties, this time, Lucio Fontana's Concetti Spaziali); a bloody red wall that sets the backdrop of the scene. As in a theater, nothing in the store is real or natural: the floor has woodgrain but is made of ceramic tiles; the Fjord red stones by Moroso are soft and upholstered in fabric and leather; the biomorphic and the geometric shapes in the space are embedded in heavy, shiny lacquers or neon lighting, yet the result is noisy silence, which is indeed a statement.

mgb was commissioned to design the interior for this fashion retail store in Vancouver's Gastown neighbourhood. Principals Michael Green and Michelle Biggar, along with Vancouver artist Brent Comber, collaborated to create a minimal space for fashion and sculpture reflective of BC. The mandate was to develop a store design that supported the simple, modern, and evolving aesthetic of the brand's fashion line.

mgb introduced a few simple design moves to the store in an effort to compliment the elegant aesthetic of the heritage shell space. Of note was the artistic collaboration of the architects and artist on a broken timber counter with intersecting white solid surface folds for jewelry, a tea bar and a sales area. In addition to the architectural and interior design of the retail space, mgb was also responsible for every aspect of the store's interior. This included the development of three custom light fixtures built in-house by the architects, and the creation of custom hangers. Other unique attributes include two circular change rooms which incorporate floor to ceiling fabric curtains instead of fixed walls; a design that allows for an open store when the rooms are not in use, and provides a soft counterpoint to the heritage brick interior when the rooms are engaged.

OBAKKI

mgb

Design/ mcfarlane green biggar Architecture+Design
Collaborator/ Brent Comber Originals Inc.
Client/ Obakki
Photography/ Scott Morgan
Site/ Vancouver, Canada
Area/ 510 sqm
Date of Completion/ 2006

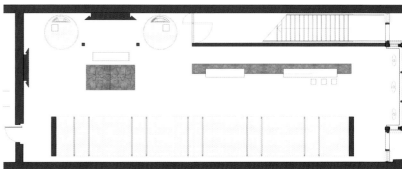

The shop is organized on two floors with 80sqm on street level and 70sqm on the lower level. On the street level, the main display and reception space is a dark gallery-like space with a central white stair element leading down to the sewing workshop. The geometry of its walls is angled to create movement and to envelope the central white spiral. Nine selected dresses are suspended, hovering from the ceiling around the monolithic staircase. Each dress is lit with a single spot, hanging on vintage-like, custom made seamstress mannequins.

The complete dress collection of approximately 150 dresses is archived in an illuminated translucent built-in glass cupboard spanning the length of one wall.

A second volume, a bridal dressing room, is kept completely white and accessed via a large cut-out in the wall of the main gallery. The room accommodates the bride and her bridal entourage.

A third room, Hila Gaon's private office, is hidden behind a pivot door. The white staircase leads to the lower level workshop where the dresses are fitted on the brides during the process of production. The lower floor accommodates the seamstresses, the cutter, storage, a kitchen and a laundry room.

The walls and ceiling in the first space are textured in dark gray shadows, resembling 30 black and white glamour photo-shoots of divas, an inspiration from one of Gaon's catalogues. The floating dresses are analogous to the bride's dream-like state of mind on the day of her marriage, and the spot light reminds one of being the star for a day. The vintage furniture is selected from flea markets and antique shops. k1p3 architects are responsible for the complete concept design and planning as well as the branding of the shop done in collaboration with graphic designer Nurit Koniak.

HILA GAON

k1p3 architects

Design/ Karina Tollman, Philipp Thomanek
Client/ Hila Gaon
Photography/ Arden Barhama
Site/ Tel Aviv, Israel
Area/ 150 sqm
Date of Completion/ 2008

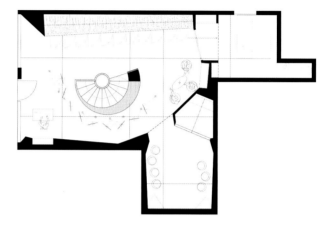

The interior design is for a Patrick Cox shop which sells bags, leather goods and accessories.

The shop is in a 17-story building, in the fashion-centric Aoyama district, Tokyo. It is located only a few steps away from the building's main entrance.

Lighting is an important aspect of the shop. The products shine and have a better look if the light source is close by, not shining down from the ceiling. So the designer positioned each cylindrical steel pendant fixture directly over a corresponding display pedestal. These fixtures provide most of the lighting in the space without the lighting from the ceiling. As a result, the space has unique conditions such as "dark above and well-lit below."

The gradation of the wall promotes this hue change from ceiling to floor. At the same time, the pendant fixtures cut the void and shape the space.

Pathways in the shop seem to meander beneath a canopy formed by the largest of the drum shades.

PATRICK COX

Sinato

Design/ Chikara Ohno
Client/ BLBG Co., Ltd.
Photography/ Toshiyuki Yano, Nacasa & Partners Inc.
Site/ Tokyo, Japan
Area/ 79 sqm
Date of Completion/ March 2009

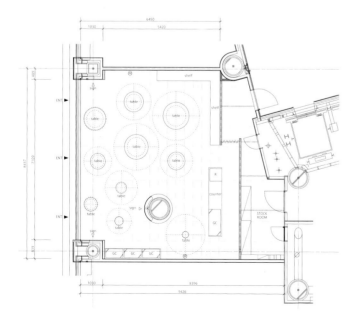

The interior of the Fumo store in Warsaw, Poland, was designed and renovated in express fashion. The name "Fumo" is a nimble set of syllables that mean nothing in Polish though they intimate "I smoke" in Spanish (fumar- yo fumo). It evokes Spanish associations, as the majority of apparel sold in the store is Spanish brands. Meanwhile, the smoke motif fits well with the slightly alternative feel of the place.

The goal was to assure that the interior of the store would attract passersby. The designers tried to expose the original terrazzo and used the most inexpensive materials, such as plywood, polycarbonate, wood paneling and, finally, fiberboard and Styrofoam. The changing room, countertop and all furniture are all made from plywood. The changing rooms are bolted together using raw plywood. The shelves disclose the plywood structure, a 20 cm block of layered plywood, which looks like a giant waffle. Accessories are displayed on the shelves and pieces of clothing hanging on a galvanized gaspipe and lighted hangers.

Inspired by the kitschy hit of Polish block housing from the 1980s with cheap wood paneling, designers arranged the boards on the wall in a strong diagonal pattern, referencing current popular trends in graphic art.

Designers used Styrofoam to make the furniture in the store. Inside the counter are shelves and drawers of fiberboard, while the countertop itself is lacquered fiberboard.

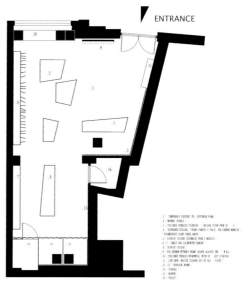

FLOOR PLAN

FUMO

Super Super & Moko Architects

Design/ Hanna Kokczynska, Jacek Majewski, Michal Gratkowski
Client/ FUMO
Photography/ Robert Ceranowicz
Site/ Warsaw, Poland
Area/ 55 sqm
Date of Completion/ January 2009

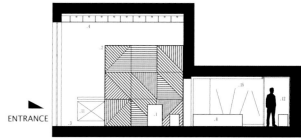

ENTRANCE

VIEW OF THE WALL WITH WOODPANELLING

The concept for the Rosato Retail Design Stores derives from the brand's slogan "Gold is Glam."

The Studio wanted the space to resemble a very luxurious, glamorous gold mine. The white ceramic walls have an organic form as if handmade. On the surface are organic shaped "holes" carved out to form the display window. The rest of the walls and ceiling are made of gold leaf; the floor is covered with off white colored moquette; the lighting is very soft and elegant; all lighting fixtures are hidden.

In the center of the room there is a cascade of gold "particles" coming down from the ceiling as if the elaborated gold was excavated from the walls.

All of the materials used are precious materials that reflect the use of gold, silver and diamonds in jewelry. Some of the products are inspired by the idea of one of a kind, handmade products, and the space similarly appears to be molded by hand. The space is very clean and glamorous.

ROSATO

Studio 63 Architecture + Design

Design/ Piero Angelo Orecchioni, Massimo Dei, Federico Gigetti
Client/ Rosato
Photography/ Yael Pincus
Site/ Milan, Italy
Area/ 20 sqm
Date of Completion/ October 2007

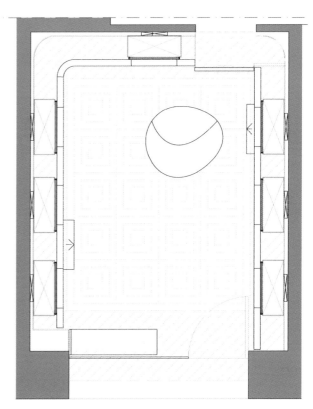

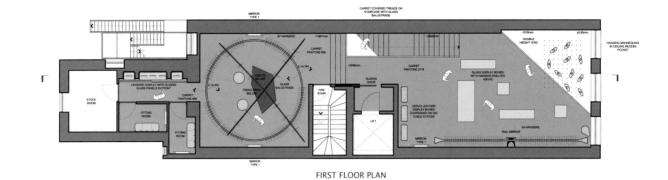

FIRST FLOOR PLAN

GROUND FLOOR PLAN

Marni's new flagship boutique is a stylized take on a gallery of modern art, reflecting the vibrant, bustling and funky atmosphere that is the New York aesthetic. Extending over two floors, abstract shapes and strong lines provide a dramatic backdrop, while sculptural forms display the collection like pieces of art.

Creating a powerful double-height entrance, a hole is punched through the ceiling into the first floor, an effect repeated at the back of the shop, allowing a giant stainless steel tree to grow up through a trapezoidal opening between the floors. Large geometric cut-outs covered with stretched Barrisol fabric provide a theatrical glow from the ceilings. Inspired by the angular simplicity of origami, polished stainless steel panels wrap around the interior walls, anchoring the space. Massive clusters of hanging mannequin pieces are scattered randomly, while backlit fiberglass accessories boxes, circular tiered shoe displays and stylized sunglass-wearing heads provide interesting focal points for the visitor.

While the materials palette of mirror-polished stainless steel, natural fiberglass and luxurious leather is intentionally quite minimalist, the effect is softened by plush carpeting throughout in varying tones of lilac.

MARNI
MADISON NYC

Sybarite

Client/ Marni, Milan, Italy
Photography/ Paul Warchol
Site/ New York, US
Area/ 250 sqm
Date of Completion/ April 2009

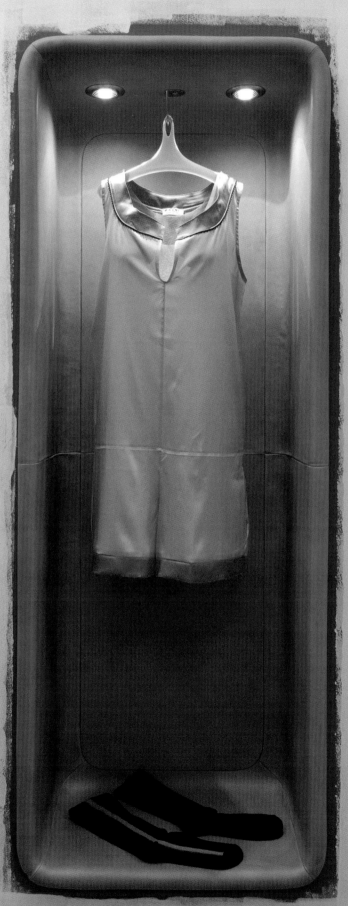

The new design for the Shoebox store in Wheatley Plaza is a combination of mainstream and offbeat. It is a surprising place rich in colors and subtleties that turn shopping into a charming experience.

A series of more than 200 wall panels of different colors and functions are installed in a grid throughout the space. Each panel, finished in either shiny lacquer, fabric or linoleum, can be repositioned on the grid, just like a pixel on a screen. Virtually thousands of different combinations of colors and materials are possible, giving the store not only the fully functional flexibility always needed in the retail industry but also the possibility of creating different moods just by combining colors and materials.

The center of the store is a seating area and display unit lit by a series of Paolo Rizzatto's Costanza lamps that help giving the feeling of a home to the space while at the same time winking at the world of Italian design, a reference always present in the projects of the Studio.

SHOEBOX

Sergio Mannino Studio

Concept Design/ S. Mannino, F. Bruni, F. Scalettaris
Client/ The Camuto Group, Nexcen
Photography/ Sergio Mannino Studio
Site/ New York, US
Area/ 150 sqm
Date of Completion/ October 2009

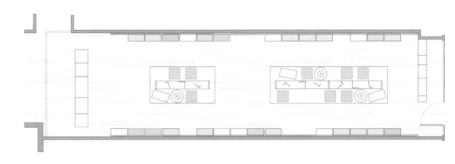

The "Leave Your Mark" concept for Alu 2007 is street art meeting high end fashion. This year's showroom is all about leaving your mark, showcasing the Alu products using materials from the forthcoming catalogue. Stencil art and handwriting on top of real life renderings make this something special. A red square was created in the center of the showroom with custom made markers for visitors to leave their mark directly on the Alu products. Also, the stencil logo is an image sprayed around the office, which works together with the graphics and patterns designed for the concept. A fantastic photo shoot is tarnished with graffiti-like lettering and it becomes a sexy mix of photography and illustration.

ALU NY SHOWROOM

Bleed

Client/ Alu S.p.a.
Photography/ Chris Harrison
Site/ New York, US
Date of Completion/ Autumn 2006

Villa Moda is a multi-brand luxury fashion store founded by Sheikh Majed, one of the driving forces behind fashion in the Middle East. For the interior design of Villa Moda, its designer Marcel Wanders found inspiration in the traditional souk, creating a melting pot of cultures full of surprising details:

"The souk is the ultimate marketplace, a concentration of innovation and tradition, diversity and intimacy. Lose yourself in labyrinth passages and find yourself anew. We designed Villa Moda Bahrain as an international Babel of fashion, in order to share instead of divide. Meet the people of the streets; shake hands and learn each other's language."

The façade is covered in giant pearl-like spheres, a reference to Bahrain's heritage as the pearl stock market of the Middle East. Customers enter a long, narrow corridor that opens into a dramatic, high-ceilinged space with giant patterns in black and white on custom carpeting and overscale wallpaper. "We worked with craftsmen from the region and around the world," Wanders adds, "but confused them with our way of looking at these crafts; we used their expertise but asked them to do things they wouldn't normally do." A striking example is a giant sculptural flower pattern made in plaster covering the wall behind the cash desk. Other specially designed features include walls with Bisazza mosaics and custom-made carpets created in Germany.

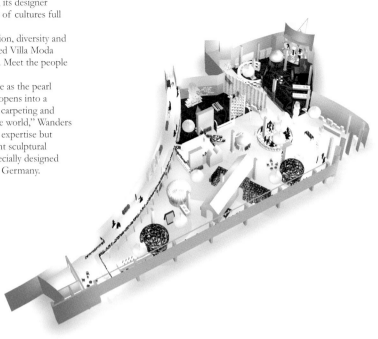

VILLA MODA

Marcel Wanders Studio

Design/ Marcel Wanders, Karin Krautgartner, Aino Kavantera
Client/ Sheikh Majed al-Sabah
Photography/ Marcel Wanders studio
Site/ Bahrain
Area/ 1,050 sqm
Date of Completion/ June, 2008

With the new concept for Alberta Ferretti, Sybarite has developed a language of lightness and transparency, grounded by a sophisticated yet simple palette of materials to form the perfect backdrop to this collection. The key design features of the new flagship store in Los Angeles are the flexibility of the bespoke display system, the disciplined continuity of the palette and the skillful use of lighting to create an atmosphere that is as sensual, airy and ethereal as the clothes themselves.

Flexibility is achieved by a completely unique system of magnetic hangers and shelving which can be freely placed against lacquered steel panels, showing the natural and volumetric form of the clothes. The freestanding elliptical rails are made from a new "black" stainless steel. The "V" profile of the rail disguises the hanger fixings and forms a crown under which the clothes appear to float freely. Lacquered petals and mannequins appear to grow naturally out of the floor in elegant compositions, offering additional display flexibility.

The choice of materials is restrained and deliberate. The hard surfaces of Perspex, steel, concrete, plaster and fiberglass are all polished or lacquered, with the reflective properties enhanced. Lighting is used to optimum effect in this design. Bearing graceful stripes of mirrored steel, the Perspex screens are both transparent and reflective, casting interesting shadows, permitting the flow of light, and creating a mood at once surreal and understated, an effect enhanced by the reflectiveness of the surface finishes. Integral LED lights in the steel rails direct attention to the hanging garments, accentuating texture, and literally highlighting the beauty and sensuality of the Alberta Ferretti collection.

ALBERTA FERRETTI

Sybarite

Client/ Alberta Ferretti
Photography/ Jimmy Cohrssen
Site/ Los Angeles, US
Area/ 400 sqm
Date of Completion/ November 2008

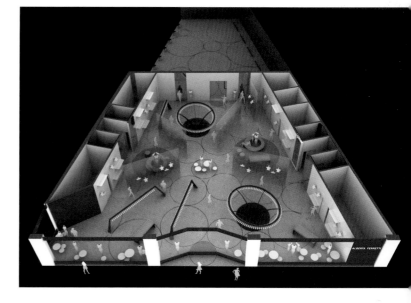

The new Ami-e-toi shop in Arnhem exudes an unmistakably luxurious style. It is the glamour style of the 1920s and 1930s, a period full of expectation in which the avant-garde flourished in art and culture. This turning point in history also characterises the fashion label Ami-e-toi, designed by young Dutch fashion designers. The collection is characterised by the modern interpretation of old forms.

The same meeting of contrasts is found in the interior, designed by the Dutch interior designer Maurice Mentjens. The straight lines of the concrete construction are softened by loosely hanging net curtains, shiny objects and two enormous mirror walls. As the long clothes rack is clamped between the mirrors at right angles, the mirror images are doubled. The collection is endlessly repeated, in all its glory and attractiveness; the ultimate fata morgana for the true fashionista. The hidden message of "a second chance" is incorporated into all the details, reflecting Mentjens' fascination with symbolism. "The wall of mirrors is not a fata morgana but the illusion of the 'fashion addict'. The chandelier made of cut glass and attached to the mirror wall is intended as a piece of pop art, with its chalice form a reference to the Holy Grail. In the world of philosophy, the Holy Grail is often defined as the spiritual search for one's true self, in which mind, body and soul ultimately come together. The same paradigm is incorporated into the monumental semi-circular table. Only through reflection and acceptance of the self-image does the whole entity emerge. This is a beautiful metaphor with the same significance for both the 'fashion victims' and the women working in the ateliers."

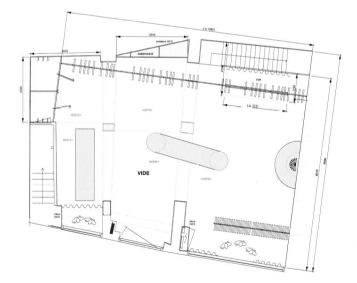

AMI-E-TOI

Maurice Mentjens Design

Client/ Mode met een Missie, Arnhem
Photography/ Arjen Schmitz
Site/ Arnhem, the Netherlands
Area/ 85 sqm
Date of Completion/ June 2009

The existing shop soon proved to be too small, and was extended last year with the addition of a neighbouring premise. The long, narrow garden in between the buildings was given a glass roof. By breaking through windows and doors in the side walls, three interconnected spaces were created with seven passageways. Maurice Mentjens created a division between the women's and men's sections precisely in the middle of the central glass-roofed space, starting with the floor. One half of the floor is pure white, the other jet black: colours representing yin and yang, the feminine and the masculine. Steel trees form a reference to the Garden of Eden; white refers to virginal innocence; black is for the lost paradise: a subtle feel for mythology and the mystical is seen in all the work of the interior designer. He combined three small spaces and then divided them again into yin and yang. Back to the origins of fashion: "the mother of all the arts." Elegant versus rugged, like the intangible, graceful world of Venus and the earthy, black smithy of Vulcan, her husband, in Roman mythology.

The connection between the spaces is made by two sales counters, half protruding into the glass-roofed space and half into the white or black areas. Thanks to an ingenious anchoring system in the wall, the blocks are almost magically suspended in space. Only the very ends are subtly supported by a plexiglass foot.

LABELS

Maurice Mentjens Design

Client/ Labels, Sittard
Photography/ Leon Abraas
Site/ Sittard, the Netherlands
Area/ 130 sqm
Date of Completion/ December 2008

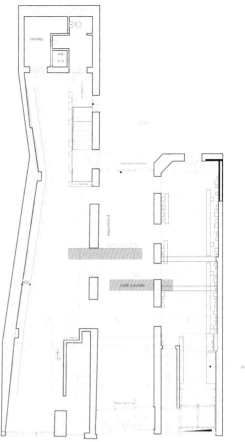

Online couture retailer Revolveclothing.com desired a flexible space for their debut physical store and the design of the boutique responds by showcasing a changing selection of designers while transforming periodically into an event space. Set back from Melrose Avenue, a square display window within a dark metal wall announces the store's entrance. Inside, a long wall of vertical fins emphasizes the space's verticality while affording individual display niches for a changing group of apparel labels. Each fin is cut to a unique curved profile, countering their repetition in the plan with a soft vertical topography. Custom designed fixtures of stainless and black dyed MDF are minimal, low, and removable. A passageway leads to a walled garden containing a set of museum-like vitrines displaying contemporary and vintage fashion pieces.

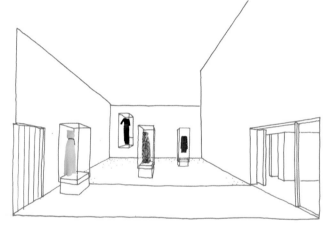

REVOLVE

Standard

Design/ Silvia Kuhle, Jeffrey Allsbrook, Moira Henry, Travis Muroki, Gregg Oelker, Caroline Smogorzewski
Client/ Revolveclothing.com
Photography/ Benny Chan
Site/ Los Angeles, US
Area/ 2,600 sqft
Date of Completion/ 2008

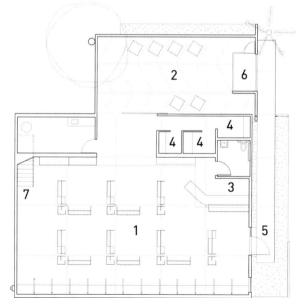

1 SHOW ROOM
2 WALLED GARDEN
3 CASH WRAP
4 DRESSING ROOMS
5 ENTRY COURTYARD
6 SHOWCASE WINDOW
7 STAIR TO UPPER SHOW ROOM

The design of the new Kensiegirl Showroom in New York City attempts to personify the chic, evocative and whimsical style of the Kensiegirl brand.

While utilizing the latest digital technologies, Mannino Studio defines the spirit of the times through mass customization of wallpapers, decals and laser-cut furniture. Through everyday fluorescent fixtures turned pink, digitally fabricated lamp shades and a display system reminiscent of 70s minimal art, the Studio was able to transform the showroom into a modern mental gymnasium of design, pattern and color, while at the same time complimenting the Kensiegirl brand.

The showroom is defined by a lighting system that emphasizes the shelving system and the display areas giving the space a theatrical effect. This is obtained not only by an accurate selection of lighting fixtures but mainly by differentiating the flooring materials: a dark navy blue carpet in the showroom in opposition to a bright "alaskan skies" concrete in the reception area.

A metal halide type of wall washer and adjustable track lights have been selected for the display shelving, where an accurate reproduction of colors and contrast was required. The front desk in the reception area is characterized by a pink fluorescent fixture reminiscent of a Dan Flavin installation. The light gives the space a touch of playfulness that plays well with the image of the brand.

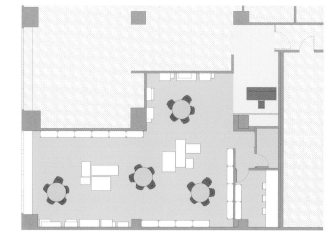

KENSIEGIRL SHOWROOM

Sergio Mannino Studio

Design/ S. Mannino, F. Scalettaris
Client/ The Camuto Group
Photography/ Sergio Mannino Studio
Site/ New York, US
Area/ 145 sqm
Date of Completion/ June 2009

The new store decor builds on Boomerang's strategic concept: "Defining Scandinavian Preppy." The aim was to design a unique, personal store which captures the Scandinavian Preppy feel without being pretentious. Another important element was developing unique details which can be incorporated into the smallest shop-in-shop outlet, creating a personality and a sense of authenticity even in a brand new space in a shopping mall.

Using the home as a metaphor influenced the choice of details, furniture, lighting, etc. to make Boomerang stand out from other store concepts. The details convey a uniquely personal feel, with pillars wrapped in Boomerang shirt fabric, specially produced rag rugs, leather-framed mirrors, images in aged frames, and ID tags on furniture and modern antiques.

It is important to create an intimate environment inside the store, capable of conveying Scandinavian Preppy while also reinforcing the feeling of a home. New furniture is partnered with design classics of the past and second-hand finds, while the color scheme, combinations of materials and the details are vital to its contemporary look. The flow inside the store uniquely emphasizes similarities with the home. Instead of being set to one side against a wall, the till, for example, is positioned out in the middle of the store, more like a desk or kitchen table than the ordinary counter. The position of the till gives staff an overview of the whole store, bringing them more directly into contact with the customer.

The lighting plays a major role in creating atmosphere, with different zones of the store lit in different ways. Lighting is also crucial in highlighting the cabinets as the main display surfaces.

The store layout is created using furniture rather than building walls. The fitting room, for example, is constructed out of folding partitions with mirrors, reminiscent of a dressing room.

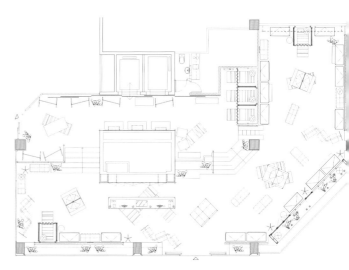

BOOMERANG FLAGSHIP STORE

Koncept

Client/ Boomerang International AB
Photography/ Mikael Fjellström
Site/ Stockholm, Sweden
Area/ 200 sqm
Date of Completion/ 2008

The Studio has extensively remodeled the Grade II former Lefevre Gallery to provide an 11,000 square foot UK headquarters incorporating 5,700 square foot of front of house retail space. Developing on the "nature abstracted" theme of the New York store, Universal has taken key structural elements and re-introduced them in a modern re-working. In other areas the fabric and finishes have been restored and are complemented by themes of nature and landscape expressed in bespoke fittings and numerous handcrafted materials.

The retail areas, designed to create a relaxed and unintimidating environment, include a perfume room, bespoke tailoring service, dedicated VIP area and garden. A monumental marquetry wall runs the length of the main retail space, incorporating a fairy tale scene designed by Stella. Contemporary furniture and fittings designed for the scheme are juxtaposed with hand-made wallpaper and hand-printed fabric walls, creating an eclectic and highly personal approach to the interior. Materials used throughout the scheme include limestone, polished black granite and smoked oak floors, structural glass, hand crafted tile walls and brushed stainless steel.

STELLA MCCARTNEY, LONDON

Universal Design Studio

Client/ Stella McCartney Ltd.
Photography/ Richard Davies, Ed Reeves
Site/ London, UK
Area/ 11,000 sqft
Date of Completion/ November 2002

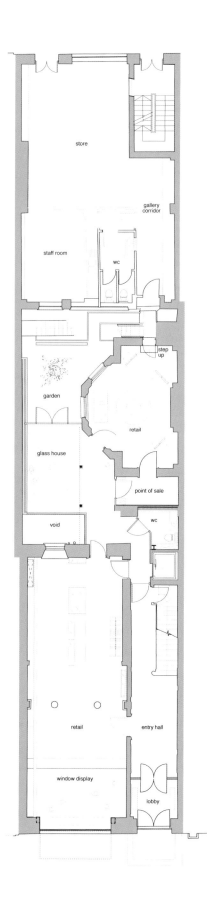

store

gallery corridor

staff room

wc

step up

garden

glass house

retail

void

point of sale

wc

retail

entry hall

window display

lobby

Universal was commissioned to deliver a full design service for Stella McCartney's US Flagship store in New York's Meat Packing district. The converted warehouse was the first in a number of Stella McCartney stores to be launched worldwide.

Stella's brief envisioned a relaxed environment with an air of nature where customers would be free to explore and discover her creations. The "abstract landscape" was informed by Stella's desire to display her collections in an environment which provided a respite from the city. The concept developed by Universal also formalized ideas about tranquility and relaxation, both of which are associated with nature. The notion of "the landscape" was realized in a series of elements of differing scales including the contours and levels of the floors and hanging screens evocative of long grass. These formed a terrain for customers to casually explore.

Another key element was the interior wall of three dimensional tiles, inspired by the hexagon, nature's building block. The tile, created by Universal's sister company, BarberOsgerby, has become a signature feature in the fashion designer's flagship stores. BarberOsgerby saw the layering of a petal motif over the hexagon as a more literal reference to the abstracted landscape theme. The pattern also offers a third visual layer, with the petals abstracting to circles when viewed from a distance. Three shapes are visible when the tiles are put together: the hexagons, the star shapes of the flower petals, and the circles which are created where the tiles overlap. The unique design had a textural, 3-D relief aspect suitable for both interior and exterior use.

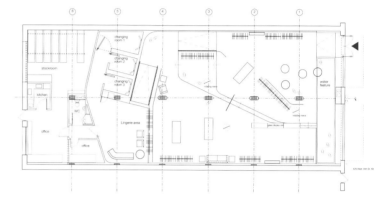

STELLA MCCARTNEY
US FLAGSHIP STORE

Universal Design Studio

Client/ Stella McCartney Ltd.
Photography/ Frank Oudeman
Site/ New York, US
Area/ 4,000 sqft
Date of Completion/ February 2002

In the autumn of 2008 Universal Design Studio created the first flagship store for United Arrows' new brand, Franqueensense in Tokyo.
The store concept created by Universal articulates the brand attitude of "approachable luxury" as two distinct environments holding two complimentary collections: "Precious" and "Easy." These two atmospheres intertwine to create one store.
The "Precious" environment is defined by a floating screen of circular lenses, a modern interpretation of the chandelier. The screen delicately refracts light and generates shifting views of the merchandise, the customers and the surrounding Aoyama street scenes. The screen has become a strong and recognizable identity holder for the Franqueensense brand.
The material palette of "Precious" reflects a luxurious atmosphere; polished brass, soft carpets in dusky pink hues, polished marble and brightly anodized aluminum.
The "Easy" area is a simpler and more informal space inspired by the modern salon. A deliberately relaxed material palette has been used to challenge that of the "Precious" area. The walls and furniture are mainly white and reflect a more functional aesthetic. The floor is walnut board edged with brass trim where it meets the carpeted shapes of the precious zone.
The shop is comprised of two floors with a total area of 2,500 square feet.

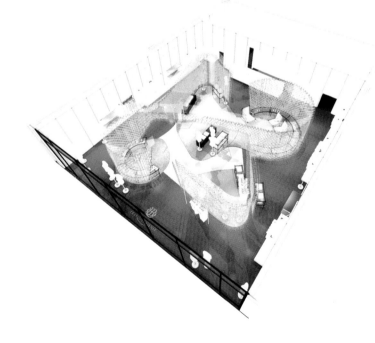

FRANQUEENSENSE

Universal Design Studio

Client/ United Arrows
Photography/ Nacasa & Partners Inc.
Site/ Tokyo, Japan
Area/ 2,500 sqft
Date of Completion/ Autumn 2008

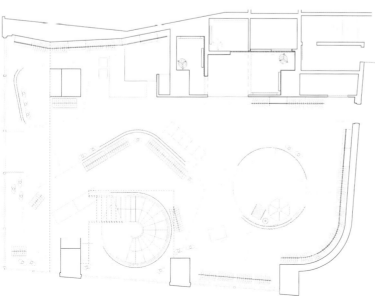

Maggy's Mode is a women's fashion retailer, which offers a huge collection to a diverse audience, ranging from young women to young grannies. Warmth, femininity, color locale, and, of course, the newest trends in fashion turn out to have an immediate strong appeal on existing as well as new customers.

The shop's large ground plan consists of two main departments, reflecting the various fashion styles preferred by the customer base. Two catwalks form a logical division of the space, their wide wooden walkways doubling as stages for fashion shows. Using shades of brown and contrasts in color and light, the store manages to emanate warmth and femininity, while offering a truly sheltered atmosphere. Unusual elements in the interior are the walls of gabions filled with wood blocks, on which sets of clothing can be presented. The enormous lampshades feature historical scenes from Spakenburg fishery life.

The whole interior consists of moveable modules that can be rearranged at will.

MAGGY'S MODE

Dastro
Retailconcepts

Client/ Maggy's Mode
Photography/ Ard Smith, Patrick Meis
Site/ Spakenburg, the Netherlands
Area/ 400 sqm
Date of Completion/ February 2009

A dramatic redesign of Wish Atlanta marks the advent of the store's evolution from hipster outpost into a sophisticated purveyor of some of the world's most cutting-edge labels. With its re-launch in September 2007, Atlanta's style elite will be able to find the highly sought-after, limited edition footwear brands which have formed the bastion of Wish's identity, alongside unique, handpicked fashion pieces from international designers under one new and exciting roof.

The main floor of the former public library is dominated by an inserted skin of raw construction plywood covering the walls and floor, in stark contrast to the original cornicing details in the existing architecture. Against this skin is a chaotic, interwoven series of shocking, chromatic tubes, which act as the merchandise railing system. The effect is dramatic and unmistakably jarring: a crazy mess of electric cables, artfully refined.

The entrance is a lit catwalk of glass boxes set into the floor which displays merchandise beneath the visitor's feet and illumination of the store is provided by a grid of suspended light bulbs hanging in regular symmetry throughout the space. Try-on rooms stand in a block of acid-etched mirror with a jewel-like effect.

The lower level is marked by its purposeful lack of natural light creating a theatrical atmosphere. Walls are covered floor to ceiling in bound books in irreverent homage to the building's distinguished past. A high gloss black ceiling and floor provides the staged backdrop for glowing glass cubes that give the shoes the celebrity status they deserve.

WISH

Established

Design/ Sam O'Donahue
Client/ Lauren Amos, Wish Atlanta
Photography/ Michael Moran
Site/ Atlanta, US
Area/ 448 sqm
Date of completion/ September 2007

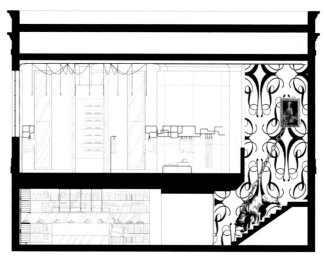

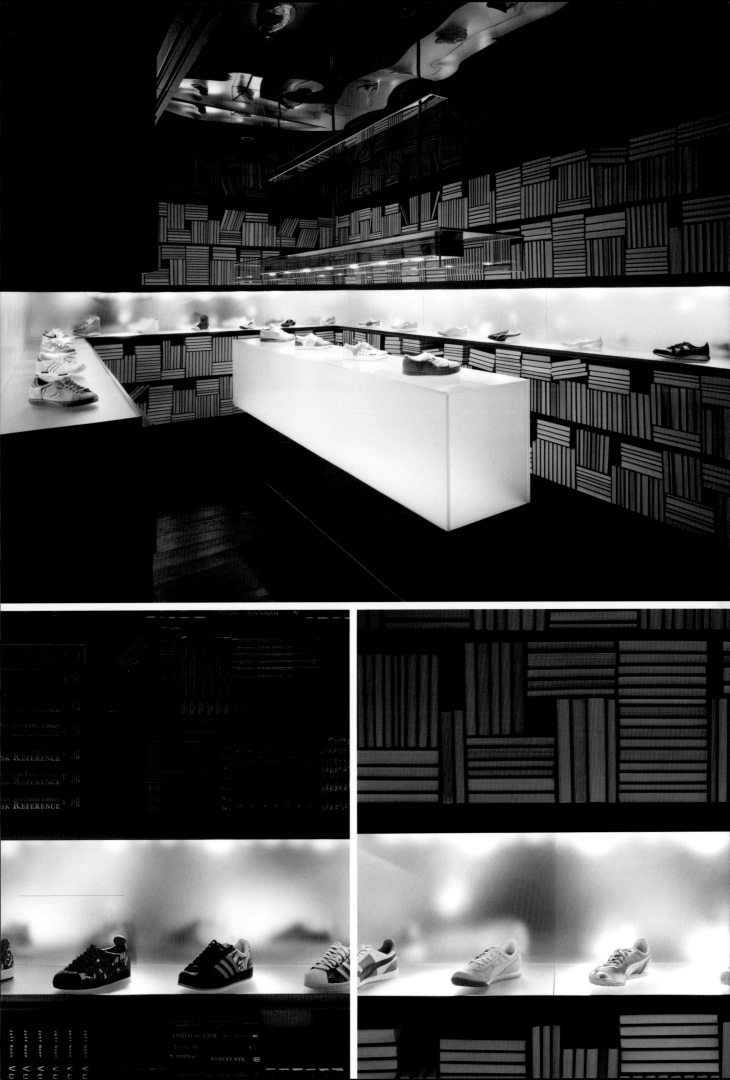

The Designer Collections Floor at Holt Renfrew's Toronto Flagship encourages shoppers to set aside all preconceived notions of what a luxury retailer should look like and provides a truly distinct retail environment.

Burdifilek's interior concept displays Holt Renfrew's collection of luxury clothing labels in a pure and complex palette of whites. The focus is on evolving the luxury shopping experience and infusing a sense of art and drama into fashion retailing. Tones of snow, pearl and alabaster play out in sculptural forms and textural materials. 40,000 pristine white rods hang in suspended animation from circular ceiling coves and sway gently, creating an ethereal backdrop.

The hanging sculptural installation evokes ultra feminine volumes, creates a point of memory and inspires the imagination. The circular forms compartmentalize the collections; clothing is displayed on brushed steel floor-mounted fixtures, hanging in unison with the ceiling details. This space not only looks, but feels a million miles away from the outside world, and emphasizes a richly indulgent experience.

A sculptural screen of clear and sandblasted Lucite cubes falls poetically from openings in the ceiling. The installations are bathed in white light and the diffused illumination creates an artistic and ethereal perception of the space. Throughout the floor, different feature tables function as display for the product, but act as art pieces as well. Solid oak dry-brushed in gold, aubergine stained Tay wood and porcelain finished wall details all contribute to the highly detailed architectural expression. Burdifilek achieves a level of international luxury retailing while merging sculpture and environment. The firm successfully created a space that is distinctly Holt Renfrew but that doesn't overpower their luxury fashion collections. The design clearly reinforces the 150 year old brand's continued commitment to premiere luxury retailing.

HOLT RENFREW

Burdifilek

Design/ Diego Burdi, Paul Filek
Client/ Holt Renfrew
Photography/ Ben Rahn, A Frame
Site/ Toronto, Canada
Area/ 16,160 sqft
Date of Completion/ September 2006

The newly created store by Deardesign Studio from Barcelona is a space of contrasts.

The store is divided into two clearly defined areas which link every technical aspect of a clothes store behind a "wooden skin" and keep clothes as the main focus. The project seeks to preserve the common characteristics of the brand's existing spaces: industrial, different and minimalistic, adding a touch of the contemporary in its architecture. The principal idea was to open the space and allow a view onto the shopping mall's park, which gives clients the sensation of shopping in a space full of natural light, as if they were in a street store. Here the Studio applies the philosophy, interpreting the act of buying in a mall as a "shopping avenue."

The park is another decorative piece of the interior. From the park the back façade attract clients in the same commercial way as the interior façade of the shopping centre. Therefore the Studio decided to bring together all the technical functions of the store (storage, fitting rooms, electrical quarter, and a second small window) in a huge unique wood structure made from 1000 pieces of wood and put together with 2400 screws. The wooden skin allows all large structures to be hidden, therefore leaving the roof clear.

From its interior, the "skin" reveals to visitors all of its extremely technical constructive secrets, bringing to mind fabric, turn-ups, stitching, etc. This reflects the real importance of technicity in clothes making and enhancing the concepts transmitted by the brand: simplicity, purity, and industry.

The installation made of irregular triangles appears rocklike like a contemporary cave. The natural beech wood stands in contrast with the opposite wall, made of concrete. Each triangle is unique and numbered to make the construction easier.

Most existing stores of the brand preserve traces of the history of the buildings. The project aims at respecting the original context and reinforcing the industrial characteristics of the building. Basic materials such as concrete for the walls and fine cement on the floor are used. These simple materials simplify the architectural reading of the store and strengthen the concept.

LURDES BERGADA

Deardesign Studio

Design/ Ignasi Llauradó, Eric Dufourd, Dorien Peeters
Client/ Lurdes Bergada & Syngman Cucala
Photography/ Pol Cucala
Site/ Barcelona, Spain
Area/ 63 sqm
Date of Completion/ August 2009

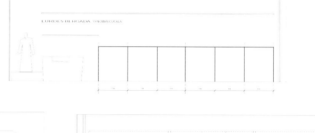

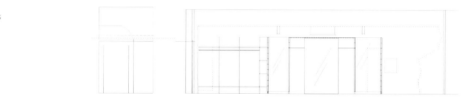

This project was created with a precise mix of traditional and contemporary, with references to art accompanying the visitor throughout the three floor store. It is an architectural box both liberating and revealing in its structure. The structure becomes part of the atmosphere. The concept of an art gallery on the ground floor and the materials to use to create it were carefully researched, and various artists worked together on location, as in a workshop. Walls were considered canvases, counters were considered sculptures, and graffiti was employed throughout the space. Materials such as iron, cement, stone, and wood accompany the art works.

PULZELLI

Studio 63
Architecture + Design

Client/ Pulzelli
Photography/ Yael Pincus
Site/ Monte S.Savino, Italy
Area/ 900 sqm
Date of Completion/ September 2007

Octium, a high concept jewelry shop, opened its doors in
October 2009. Located in 360° mall in Kuwait, Octium presents
the work of various exclusive jewelry designers from around
the globe. Hayón's design offers an innovative approach to the
interior. Most elements were custom designed for the project
using contrasting finishes like glossy lacquered woods, natural
oak, ceramic and luxurious fabrics.

OCTIUM JEWELRY

Hayón Studio

Design/ Jaime Hayón
Client/ Octium
Photography/ Hayón Studio
Site/ Kuwait
Date of Completion/ October 2009

1:2:3 & Kristoffer Sundin

1:2:3 is a design firm based in Stockholm, sweden while Kristoffer Sundin is an interior designer based in Stockholm, Sweden. They work together with projects that they think require each other's knowledge. Their goal is to work in a way that allows their different fields of design to work together as one, resulting in something new and hopefully better.

www.1-2-3info.se
www.kristoffersundin.se

Alfredo Häberli

Alfredo Häberli was born in Buenos Aires, Argentina, in 1964. Today, he is an internationally established designer based in Zurich. He manages to unite tradition with innovation, joy and energy in his designs. He has a wide range of clients, such as Alias, Camper, Iittala, Kvadrat, Luceplan, Moroso and Volvo.

www.alfredo-haeberli.com

Andrea Tognon Architecture

Andrea Tognon Architecture is an architectural and communication design research laboratory founded in 2002. It aims at understanding and developing strategies of communication and branding, modeling and transforming spaces, defining identity in the dynamic process of the complexity of urban situations. The firm combines practice with research in a multi-disciplinary approach while drawing upon a network of creative, technical and engineering firms, who integrate different aspects of the design process and construction. Over the years there have been collaborations with companies like Bottega Veneta, Krizia, Tod's, Lamarthe, Stiletto NYC, ATO APO, Tognon Arredamenti and others.

www.atognon.com

blazysgérard

In 2003, Alexandre Blazys and Benoît Gérard joined their talents and knowledge to create an office of design and architecture. Their goal is to create balanced, functional and useful human environments, in order to offer the users a new emotional and artistic appreciation of the physical and built surrounding in which they evolve.

www.blazysgérard.com

Bleed

Bleed is a multi-disciplinary design consultancy based in Oslo, Norway, established in June 2000. Working to challenge today's conventions around art, visual language, media and identity, Bleed's work spans brand identity and development, art direction, packaging, printed matter, interactive design, art projects and exhibitions. Both their client list and creative output have become diverse and interesting, and made them one of the most awarded agencies in Norway, with international and national acclaim. Bleed believe in the power of visual language. Their work deals with long term brand-strategies as well as keeping it fresh by constantly challenging the boundaries of design and media.

www.bleed.com

Burdifilek

Burdifilek is a leading full service interior design firm. The Toronto-based company provides the creative strength behind some of the most dynamic and commercially-proven global retail and hospitality environments. Its work spans the creation

of multiple award-winning flagships, multi-store rollouts, brand launches and brand evolutions from upper mass-market to luxury.

The Burdifilek design philosophy embrace creative intelligence. Burdifilek's unique design identity is demonstrated through a wide range of national and international projects that offer brand-strategic, creative sophisticated solutions.

With a staff of 35 employees, the 15 year old company is headed by Managing Partner Paul Filek, and Creative Partner Diego Burdi.

www.burdifilek.com

CASE-REAL

Koichi Futatsumata was born in Kagoshima, Japan, in 1975. He studied in the Department of Architecture, within the school of technology at Kyushu Sangyo University in 1998. In 2000, he established his design firm CASE-REAL, now based in Fukuoka and Tokyo. Thereafter, he was involved in a variety of design activities such as architecture, furniture design and products design based on the design space. His design work stems from his unique sense of modeling and features elaborate details, as well as artificial roughness. It is always simple, quiet, and powerful.

www.casereal.com
www.futatsumata.com

Curiosity

Curiosity is a design firm establishewd by Gwenael Nicolas in Tokyo.

The portfolio includes interior design, package design, graphics and advertising. Gwenael Nicolas, the Frenchman with the British design education and his partner, Reiko Myamoto with her advertising background embrace the world with a foothold not only in Tokyo, but also in New York and Paris.

www.curiosity.jp

Dastro Retailconcepts

Dastro Retailconcepts is a design agency whose name clearly highlights the firm's core business: retail design. Dastro has gathered experience in various branches of the industry thanks to projects for fashion, shoe, perfume and jewelry stores; pharmacies; opticians; and spaces belonging to the automotive and telecom sectors.

www.dastro.nl

Deardesign Studio

Deardesign was founded in the year 2005 by Ignasi Ilaurado and Eric Dufourd.

Deardesign is the result of adding, to the expertise of its partners and contributors, the contemporary design objective: functionality and pleasure.

The Deardesign team is composed of professionals in interior, graphic and industrial design. They share a very ambitious challenge: to conceive creativity as a whole. The suppression of barriers between art and technique is the motor of this philosophy.

This is how Deardesign offers coherent and global solutions to projects, not just for companies but also for private individuals.

The Deardesign innovative spirit can be seen in corporate images, in the creation and refurbishment of architectural spaces and also in the design of products and venues.

Deardesign offers to national and international clients adaptive solutions within their market areas, such as market study, branding, brand positioning and global communication. Its clients include Burberry, Nike, Munich, Lurdes Bergada, LVMH.

www.deardesign.net

Elevation Workshop

Elevation Workshop (ELEV) is an interdisciplinary Architecture and Design Firm. Positioned at the crossroads of art and architecture, the firm's interests range from urban and rural planning, architectural design to furniture and product design. The founding partners, Na Wei and Christopher W. Mahoney come from different backgrounds and foundations to create an interactive environment with a broad perspective.

www.elevationworkshop.com

Established

As both an industrial and interior designer, Sam O'Donahue, founder of Established, has been responsible for designing award-winning bottles and packaging for such clients as Evian, Estee Lauder and Allied Domecq. His interior design projects include work for top international clients such as BMW and Diesel and O'Donahue was behind the widely published redesign of New York's famed Limelight nightclub.

www.establishedny.com

Franklin Azzi Architecture

Franklin Azzi Architecture is a multicultural team of professionals from diverse backgrounds varying from architectural and interior design to town planning and graphic design.

Main projects undertaken include the Bali Barret's shops in Japan, the complex of Cinema in Tirana, Albania and the Lido club in Shanghai, China.

www.franklinazzi.com

Guise

The Swedish firm Guise was originally founded as DRD-A by Andreas Ferm and Jani Kristoffersen in 2003. The company Guise approaches commissions with a subjective reading of every individual project's brief. The formal language spans from strict simplistic geometries to complex and dynamic shapes. The ambition is to let every project generate intricate form that handles both functional needs as well as to offer strong spatial experiences to its users.

www.guise.se

Hayón Studio

Spanish artist-designer Jaime Hayón was born in Madrid in 1974. As a teenager he submerged himself in skateboard culture and graffiti art, the foundation of the detailed, bold-yet-whimsical designs so distinctive in his work today. After studying industrial design in Madrid and Paris he joined Fabrica in 1997, working closely with legendary image maker and agitator Oliverio Toscani. In a short time he was promoted to the head of their design department, where he oversaw projects ranging from shops, restaurants, exhibition displays and designs to graphics. In 2004, Hayón Studio was founded.

www.hayonstudio.com

HUGE Architects

Huge is an international multidisciplinary design firm that has more than 10 years of experience within China and abroad. HUGE has a support network of designers, collaborating experts and its own collective experience of over 15 years working in Australia, the Netherlands, the United

Kingdom, Germany, The Middle East, Indonesia and China.

The HUGE team is a mix of cultural backgrounds and experience across all design platforms. HUGE has provided design services to a wide range of clientele including the municipal government, public institutions and private developers on various building typologies including industrial parks, commercial buildings, sports venues and mixed-use residential developments.

www.hugeshanghai.com

k1p3 architects

K1p3 architects is a young architectural practice involved mainly in retail and residential planning as well as some artist collaborations. The studio is led by architects Karina Tollman and Philipp Thomanek, and is based in Tel Aviv, Israel.

www.k1p3architects.com

Koncept

Koncept was created by Ann-Marie Ekroth, Cecilia Clase, Ulf maxe, Paola Padoan and Nils Nilsson.

A high level of creativity, combined with experience gained from 700 projects is how Koncept guarantees results. It approached work with joy and enthusiasm. They are well organized and deliver what they promise.

Koncept is active in Sweden and internationally. Since its founding, it has completed projects in more than 20 countries.

www.koncept.se

Marcel Wanders Studio

The studio was established by Marcel Wanders, the Dutch industrial designer known as one of the designers of Droog design. The studio designs for a global market and focuses on product and interior design. The studio is divided into product design and interior design teams and employs approximately 35 people from 11 countries. The studio is based in Amsterdam.

www.marcelwanders.com

Maurice Mentjens Design

Maurice Mentjens designs interiors, interior objects, furniture and exhibition concepts. Nearly all the firm's realized projects are in the retail, hospitality and office sectors. Years of experience has not diminished a preference for small-scale projects with a focus on quality and creativity. The firm has won three Dutch design awards (interior design) and in 2007 the Design Award of the Federal Republic of Germany. Its aim is to realize high-quality designs with a small but dynamic team of enthusiastic and talented staff members. Clients include the Bonnefanten Museum Maastricht, Frans Hals Museum Haarlem, DSM and Solland Solar Heerlen and Post Panic Amsterdam.

www.mauricementjens.com

mgb

Mcfarlane Green Biggar ARCHITECTURE + DESIGN (mgb) is a multi-disciplinary architecture and design firm based in North Vancouver, British Columbia, Canada. mgb believes that enduring architecture is the only architecture. The firm is a champion

of a new sustainable aesthetic, one where modesty trumps fanfare. The consumer age of architecture is over. Efficient, simple buildings that use less energy and create less waste - this is the goal of each mgb project. For design is not complete when there is nothing more to add. It is complete when there is nothing more to take away.

www.mgb-architecture.ca

Nendo

Oki Sato was born in Canada in 1977 and in 2002 completed his Masters in Architecture in Waseda University, Tokyo. He first started his studio "Nendo" in Tokyo and later established an office in Milan. He received numerous accolades in the field. In 2003, he won the Tokyo Designers Block Award; in 2004, he received Japanese Society of Commercial Space Designers Rookie Award, Good Design Award, ELLE DECO International Design Award and so on.

www.nendo.jp

Pierre Jorge Gonzalez / Judith Haase / ZAS

Founded in 1999, Pierre Jorge Gonzalez and Judith Haase opened their architectural firm in Berlin and Paris. The principal practices are architecture, design, scenography and lighting.

In New York working with Richard Gluckman and Robert Wilson for his Watermill Center provided a first occasion to consider ways of presenting art through architecture.

The interaction of lighting and architecture remains a primary focus for the conception of spatial contexts for art and art.

...lated activities. The atelier has a well-
...oted reputation for its involvement with
...ntemporary artists, curators, or collectors
...create the appropriate space to feature
...artwork, a luxury product or a body
...r a performance. Examples include the
...ell known Gallery Nordenhake in Berlin
...hich has become a new model for gallery
...esign, or the Andreas Murkudis Stores...

www.plajer-franz.com

REX

...EX is an internationally acclaimed
...rchitecture and design firm based in
...ew York City. In addition to the recently
...ompleted Dee and Charles Wyly Theatre
...r the AT&T Performing Arts Center in
...allas, Texas, projects in progress by REX
...clude Museum Plaza, a 62-story mixed-
...se skyscraper housing a contemporary
...t center in Louisville, Kentucky, the new
...entral Library and Music Conservatory
...r the city of Kortrijk, Belgium, and the
...stanbul headquarters for Vakko and
...ower Media, Turkey's preeminent fashion
...nd media companies. Joshua Prince-
...amus is President of REX and Principal
... Charge of all projects. Prince-Ramus
...as the founding partner of OMA New
...ork - the American affiliate of the Office
...r Metropolitan Architecture (OMA) - and
...erved as its Principal until he renamed
...e firm REX in 2006. While REX was still
...nown as OMA New York, Prince-Ramus
...as Partner in Charge of the Guggenheim-
...ermitage Museum in Las Vegas and
...e Seattle Central Library. REX recently
...laced second in both the international
...ompetition for the new Edvard Munch
...useum in Oslo, Norway, and the Finnish
...nnovation Fund's Low2No sustainable
...evelopment competition in Helsinki,
...inland.

www.rex-ny.com

SAKO Architects

SAKO Architects was founded in 2004 by
Keiichiro Sako, ten years after he graduated
from Tokyo Institute of Technology. Based
in Beijing, Keiichiro Sako has launched
several brilliant projects in China, including
Romanticism Store in Hangzhou, Lattice
Project, Mosaic Project and Bumps in
Beijing. The most important concept for the
office is to find a theme and express it in
architecture.

www.sako.co.jp

Sergio Mannino Studio

A group of creative professionals with roots
in the Italian design culture.

Sergio Mannino Studio is located in
Brooklyn's progressive art community
of DUMBO (New York). The aesthetic
approach of each project is fresh and
playful. The studio is a collection of
forward thinking architects, interior/product
designers who bring disparate ideas and
materials together to create places and
objects that delight, enlighten and inspire.
Through an extensive close network of
consultants and partners, projects can be
taken from preliminary brainstorming to
built form virtually anywhere.

Sergio Mannino graduated in Architecture
from the University of Florence, Italy under
the direction of Ettore Sottsass and Remo
Buti. He collaborated for 3 years with
Professor Remo Buti during which time
he had the opportunity to study furniture
design and interior architecture in depth.
He designed projects for architecture and
design competitions and, with his partner
Lucia Gori, won the 2000 "Concorso
di idee per il recupero dell'Area Ex-
Longinotti, Firenze." In September 2002 he
mounted a one-man show of his furniture
designs, including 3 built-pieces and 100
watercolors, at the Memphis-Post design

Gallery in Milan, once again under Sottsass'
supervision. In New York since 2001 Sergio
has worked on several commercial and
residential projects for renowned companies
such as Miss Sixty, Energie, Breil, Jessica
Simpson, Vince Camuto, Kensiegirl and
several others.

www.sergiomannino.com

Slade Architecture

In collaboration with the clients, Slade
Architecture design spaces that merge
concept and functionality. Their approach
is at once structured and unique to the
situation; creating the design paradigm for
the specific context and need. To them,
successful projects are those that articulate
the clients' interests with simplicity and
impact. Their work has been recognized,
published and exhibited extensively in the
United States and internationally.

www.sladearch.com

Sinato

Chikara Ohno

First class registered architect of Japan

Representative director of Sinato Inc.

1976 born in Osaka, Japan

1999 graduated from the department of
civil engineering, Kanazawa University

2004 established Sinato Inc.

www.sinato.jp

Standard

Established in 1992 as an art and architecture gallery in Venice, California, Standard evolved into an informal collaboration of a small group of architects, artists and writers with shared interests in contemporary art, architecture, and the urban environment. Standard has grown into a multidisciplinary architecture and design practice.

Standard's ethos derives from the firm's mastery of craft and process and fundamental belief in collaboration. The firm's meticulous attention to detail and commitment to relationships based on dialogue, continuity and trust ensures work of high quality and integrity. Standard produces architecture that responds effectively, efficiently and succinctly to a project's context and a client's needs. Standard's designs are elemental, evocative and precise.

www.standard-la.com

Studio 63 Architecture + Design

Studio 63 Architecture + Design is based in the historical center of Florence, Italy. The fruitful encounter between Piero Angelo Orecchioni and Massimo Dei led to the foundation of Studio 63 in 1998. By 2003, Studio 63 inaugurated its New York City office, by 2005 its office in Hong Kong and by 2008 its office in Shanghai and an operative partnership in Dubai.

The creative team is composed of gifted professionals, coming from various disciplines, working together in a fertile and challenging multi-cultural exchange.

A strong identity is the hallmark of their projects. This identity is the result of extended research, creative proposals and deep respect for the contemporary language criteria.

www.studio63.it

Studio Arthur Casas

Arthur Casas graduated in 1983 from Mackenzie University in Sao Paulo with a degree in Architecture. His architectural designs cover a scope of interior, residential, commercial and new construction projects. Arthur Casas has claimed prestigious awards such as 2008 Red Dot Design Award and he continues to be an active participant in various global exhibitions. Since 2004, he has been frequently invited to speak about his architecture and design.

www.arthurcasas.com

Suppose Design Office

Makoto Tanijiri was born in Hiroshima, Japan, in 1974. In 1994, he finished his study in Anabuki Design College. Suppose Design Office was established in 2000. Makoto Tanijiri thinks that it is important to keep looking for something new as an architect. He defined his work as a chance to realize fresh ideas about buildings and relationships of all interactive elements.

www.suppose.jp

Sybarite

Sybarite is an architectural and design practice that aims to tease all of the human senses and to sculpt architecture into the living environment in which it exists, whilst retaining complete functionality. We draw our passion and inspiration from organic forms in nature as well as technologies transferred from other industries. Striking a balance between realized and experimental projects is crucial in keeping us at the top of our game.

The practice was formed in 2002 by Torquil McIntosh (right) and Simon Mitchell (left) who both believe design can and should fulfill the twin briefs of functionality and pleasure and that there should be no boundaries between art, sculpture and architecture. The word "Sybarite" encapsulates this design ethos, voluptuous, luxurious and pleasurable.

An RIBA registered practice based in London in the UK, Sybarite has representatives in major cities worldwide and is fully capable of handling geographically dispersed projects.

www.sybarite-uk.com

Tokujin Yoshioka Design

Tokujin Yoshioka was born in Saga, Japan in 1967. After worked under Shiro Kuramata and Issey Miyake, he established his own studio, Tokujin Yoshioka Design in 2000.

Tokujin has collaborated with various noted companies in and outside Japan such as Hermes, Swarovski and Issey Miyake, for which he has been doing shop design and installation.

The paper chair "Honey-pop" (2001), Yamagiwa's lighting "ToFU" and cell phone "Media Skin" for au design project have been highly evaluated as art works more than as design works and became a part of permanent collections in the world's well-known museums such as Museum of Modern Art (MoMA) in New York.

He has been awarded Mainichi Design Award, 2001, Cultural Affairs Section of Government of Japan, Encourage Prize, 2006 and Design Miami/Designer of the Year, 2007. He has also been selected as one of "100 Japanese respected by the world" in Newsweek magazine of Japanese edition.

www.tokujin.com

Universal Design Studio

Universal Design Studio is recognized as one of the world's most innovative creative design consultancies. It has a distinct, multi-disciplinary approach towards the design of branded environments. The team of architects, interior designers and product designers are committed to creating unique, arresting, comprehensive environments with effective commercial purposes.

Universal was founded in London in 2001 by its sister company Barber Osgerby to augment their award-winning product and furniture design folio. A second studio was opened in Melbourne in 2008.

www.universaldesignstudio.com

upsetters architects

Shuzo Okabe was born in Ehime, Japan, in 1980. He obtained his master degree at Keio University Graduate School of Media and Governance Environmental Design Program. In 2004, he started upsetters architects.

"Observe the city and re-construct the cityscape," declares the office's concept. The office is working on architecture, interior design, events, etc. which are related to all city activities. It has been awarded JCD Design Award Gold Prize, Good Design Awards, and so on.

www.upsetters.jp

William Russell, Pentagram

William Russell studied architecture at the University of Newcastle-upon-Tyne and the Royal College of Art, working in Hong Kong, China for commercial architects MJM between degrees. Having graduated from the RCA, he set up practice with David Adjaye before establishing William Russell Architecture & Design in 2000. In April 2005 he joined Pentagram's London

office as Partner. His recent clients have included Alexander McQueen, Cass Art, COS, Krug Champagne, the London Borough of Camden, Margaret Howell and the Tate Gallery. The construction of his own residence in Bacon Street, East London has attracted critical acclaim from around the world.

www.pentagram.com

Z-A Studio

Z-A is a New York based Studio for Design Innovation, which is dedicated to exposing the unexpected in the mundane.

Z-A explores adaptive materials, structures and infrastructures that can adjust and respond to changing needs, uses and identities of a project. Through different mediums, the economy of spatial mutations and temporal existence is explored and cultivated into s specific design tool.

Z-A gained national and international visibility through numerous awards and publications such as: Architectural Record, Frame, Wall Paper, Metropolis, We-Ar, SPA-DE, Mark, Time Out, Architect's Newspaper and Haaretz.

www.z-astudio.com

ACKNOWLEDGEMENTS

We would like to thank all the architects and designers for their kind permission to publish their works, as well as all the photographers who have generously granted us the rights to use their images. We are also very grateful to many other people whose names do not appear on the credits but who made specific contributions and support. Without them, we would not be able to share these beautiful commercial spaces with readers around the world.